One Pot

PaRragon

Bath · New York · Singapore · Hong Kong · Cologne · Delhi · Melbourne

This edition published by Parragon in 2010

Parragon Publishing
Queen Street House
4 Queen Street
Bath BA1 1HE, UK

Internal design by Terry Jeavons & Company
Additional text by Linda Doeser

ISBN 978-1-4075-9474-3

Printed in China

Notes for the Reader

This book uses imperial, metric, and U.S. cup measurements. Follow the same units of measurement throughout; do not mix imperial and metric. All spoon measurements are level: teaspoons are assumed to be 5 ml, and tablespoons are assumed to be 15 ml. Unless otherwise stated, milk is assumed to be whole, eggs and individual vegetables, such as potatoes, are medium, and pepper is freshly ground black pepper.

The times given are an approximate guide only. Preparation times differ according to the techniques used by different people and the cooking times may also vary from those given as a result of the type of oven used. Optional ingredients, variations, or serving suggestions have not been included in the calculations.

Recipes using raw or very lightly cooked eggs should be avoided by infants, the elderly, pregnant women, convalescents, and anyone with a chronic condition. Pregnant and breast-feeding women are advised to avoid eating peanuts and peanut products. People with nut allergies should be aware that some of the prepared ingredients used in the recipes in this book may contain nuts. Always check the packaging before use.

One Pot

introduction

The great thing about one-pot cooking is that it makes life easier. Everything goes into one pan or casserole, you don't have to schedule time for cooking accompaniments, and there's a lot less to clear up at the end of the meal, especially if you have oven to table cookware. However, there are other less obvious advantages, too.

Among the most popular one-pot meals are meal-in-a-bowl soups, stews, and casseroles because they are so full of flavor. They are usually made with less expensive cuts of meat, which become meltingly tender during prolonged cooking and often have a greater depth of flavor than the more expensive ones. Including plenty of

vegetables and/or beans in the dish not only adds flavor and richness, but also helps stretch the meat further, making the meal extremely economical. As a rule, most stews and casseroles don't take long to prepare and once they are simmering delectably, you can go and do something else or even relax while they cook to perfection. Conveniently, they taste even better if they are cooked in advance and reheated and they also freeze well, so if time is limited it is easy to plan ahead.

Not all one-pot dishes are slow cooked nor are they invariably hearty stews. Stir-frying—one-wok cooking—is one of the fastest ways of preparing food. It is quick and easy to add variety to the family menu with a Chinese chow mein made in minutes or an Indian or Thai curry that takes only a little longer. If you want to vary your repertoire of recipes, then try a creamy Italian risotto, a mouthwatering Spanish paella, or a Creole-style jambalaya—all delicious one-pot dishes.

Fish and seafood benefit from quick cooking and make terrific one-pot meals, whether broiled, roasted, or poached in sauce. Vegetarian dishes also tend to be speedy, especially if you use canned beans, which do not require soaking and cooking before use.

meal-in-a-bowl soups

Homemade soups are always welcome and have the added advantage of being incredibly easy to make. A meal-in-a-bowl soup is the perfect choice for a weekend lunch for busy families, especially when a lot of different activities mean that family members may be eating at different times. They can also be prepared in advance, making them ideal for a late-night supper after a long and busy day or for informal entertaining.

Soups can be hearty winter warmers or lighter, more summery dishes and may be based on vegetables, meat, poultry, or fish. For centuries, cooks around the world have recognized the nutritional and economic value of substantial soups for easy meals, basing them on local ingredients and flavors—from Italian minestrone to French onion soup.

A meal-in-a-bowl soup is a simple way to guarantee healthy eating. Meat, fish, or beans provide protein, while a mix of vegetables—the more colorful the better—supplies vitamins and minerals. Many soups contain rice, noodles, pasta, or potatoes—all good sources of slow-release carbohydrates to maintain energy levels. If they don't, just serve them with some crusty bread or rolls. You can even ladle the soup over slices of bread in the bottom of the bowls, as is often done in France and Italy.

chunky vegetable soup

ingredients

SERVES 6

2 carrots, sliced

1 onion, diced

1 garlic clove, crushed

12 oz/350 g new potatoes,
   diced

2 celery stalks, sliced

4 oz/115 g button
   mushrooms, quartered

14 oz/400 g canned chopped
   tomatoes

2$\frac{1}{2}$ cups vegetable stock

1 bay leaf

1 tsp dried mixed herbs or
   1 tbsp chopped fresh
   mixed herbs

$\frac{1}{2}$ cup corn kernels, frozen or
   canned, drained

$\frac{1}{2}$ cup shredded green
   cabbage

pepper

crusty whole-wheat or white
   bread rolls, to serve

method

1 Put the carrots, onion, garlic, potatoes, celery, mushrooms, tomatoes, and stock into a large pan. Stir in the bay leaf and herbs. Bring to a boil, then reduce the heat, cover, and let simmer for 25 minutes.

2 Add the corn and cabbage and return to a boil. Reduce the heat, cover, and let simmer for 5 minutes, or until the vegetables are tender. Remove and discard the bay leaf. Season to taste with pepper.

3 Ladle into warmed bowls and serve immediately with crusty bread rolls.

minestrone

ingredients

SERVES 4

2 tbsp olive oil

2 garlic cloves, chopped

2 red onions, chopped

$2^3/_4$ oz/75 g prosciutto, sliced

1 red bell pepper, seeded and
    chopped

1 orange bell pepper, seeded
    and chopped

14 oz/400 g canned chopped
    tomatoes

4 cups vegetable stock

1 celery stalk, trimmed and
    sliced

14 oz/400 g canned
    cranberry beans, drained

1 cup shredded green leafy
    cabbage

$^3/_4$ cup frozen peas, thawed

1 tbsp chopped fresh parsley

$2^3/_4$ oz/75 g dried vermicelli

salt and pepper

freshly grated Parmesan
    cheese, to garnish

fresh crusty bread, to serve

method

1 Heat the oil in a large pan. Add the garlic, onions, and prosciutto and cook over medium heat, stirring, for 3 minutes, until slightly softened. Add the red and orange bell peppers and the tomatoes and cook for an additional 2 minutes, stirring.

2 Stir in the stock, then add the celery, beans, cabbage, peas, and parsley. Season to taste with salt and pepper. Bring to a boil, then lower the heat and simmer for 30 minutes.

3 Add the vermicelli to the pan. Cook for an additional 10–12 minutes, or according to the package directions. Remove from the heat and ladle into serving bowls. Garnish with freshly grated Parmesan and serve with fresh crusty bread.

ribollita

ingredients

SERVES 4

3 tbsp olive oil

2 red onions, coarsely chopped

3 carrots, sliced

3 celery stalks, coarsely
  chopped

3 garlic cloves, chopped

1 tbsp chopped fresh thyme

14 oz/400 g canned cannellini
  beans, drained and rinsed

14 oz/400 g canned chopped
  tomatoes

2½ cups water or vegetable
  stock

2 tbsp chopped fresh parsley

1 lb 2 oz/500 g Tuscan kale
  or savoy cabbage,
  trimmed and sliced

1 small day-old ciabatta loaf,
  torn into small pieces

salt and pepper

extra virgin olive oil, to serve

method

1 Heat the oil in a large saucepan and cook the onions, carrots, and celery for 10–15 minutes, stirring frequently. Add the garlic, thyme, and salt and pepper to taste. Continue to cook for an additional 1–2 minutes, until the vegetables are golden.

2 Add the cannellini beans to the pan and pour in the tomatoes. Add enough of the water to cover the vegetables. Bring to a boil and simmer for 20 minutes. Add the parsley and Tuscan kale and cook for an additional 5 minutes.

3 Stir in the bread and add a little more water, if needed. The soup should be thick.

4 Taste and adjust the seasoning, adding salt and pepper if needed. Ladle into warmed serving bowls and serve hot, drizzled with extra virgin olive oil.

vegetable & corn chowder

ingredients

SERVES 4

1 tbsp vegetable oil

1 red onion, diced

1 red bell pepper, seeded
   and diced

3 garlic cloves, minced

1 large potato, diced

2 tbsp all-purpose flour

$2^1/_2$ cups milk

$1^1/_4$ cups vegetable stock

$^3/_4$ cup broccoli florets

3 cups canned corn kernels,
   drained

$^3/_4$ cup cheddar cheese,
   grated

salt and pepper

1 tbsp chopped fresh cilantro,
   to garnish

method

1 Heat the oil in a large saucepan. Add the onion, bell pepper, garlic, and potato and cook over low heat, stirring frequently, for 2–3 minutes.

2 Stir in the flour and cook, stirring, for 30 seconds. Gradually stir in the milk and stock.

3 Add the broccoli and corn. Bring the mixture to a boil, stirring constantly, then reduce the heat and simmer for about 20 minutes, or until all the vegetables are tender.

4 Stir in $^1/_2$ cup of the cheese until it melts.

5 Season to taste with salt and pepper and spoon the chowder into warmed serving bowls. Garnish with the remaining cheese and the cilantro and serve.

french onion soup

ingredients

SERVES 6

1 lb 8 oz/675 g onions

3 tbsp olive oil

4 garlic cloves, 3 chopped
    and 1 peeled and halved
    lengthwise

1 tsp sugar

2 tsp chopped fresh thyme,
    plus extra sprigs
    to garnish

2 tbsp all-purpose flour

$1/2$ cup dry white wine

8 cups vegetable stock

6 slices of French bread

3 cups grated Swiss cheese

method

1 Thinly slice the onions. Heat the oil in a large heavy-bottom pan, then add the onions and cook, stirring occasionally, for 10 minutes, until they are just beginning to brown. Stir in the chopped garlic, sugar, and thyme, then reduce the heat and cook, stirring occasionally, for 30 minutes, or until the onions are golden brown.

2 Sprinkle in the flour and cook, stirring, for 1–2 minutes. Stir in the wine. Gradually stir in the stock and bring to a boil, skimming off any foam that rises to the surface, then reduce the heat and simmer for 45 minutes.

3 Meanwhile, toast the bread on both sides under a preheated medium broiler. Rub the toast with the cut sides of the halved garlic clove.

4 Ladle the soup into 6 flameproof bowls set on a cookie sheet. Float a piece of toast in each bowl and divide the grated cheese among them. Place under a preheated medium–hot broiler for 2–3 minutes, or until the cheese has just melted. Garnish with thyme sprigs and serve.

leek & potato soup

ingredients

SERVES 4–6

4 tbsp butter

1 onion, chopped

3 leeks, sliced

2 potatoes, cut into $^3/_4$-inch/
   2-cm cubes

3$^1/_2$ cups vegetable stock

salt and pepper

$^2/_3$ cup light cream, to serve
   (optional)

2 tbsp snipped fresh chives,
   to garnish

method

1 Melt the butter in a large saucepan over medium heat, add the onion, leeks, and potatoes, and sauté gently for 2–3 minutes, until softened but not browned. Pour in the stock, bring to a boil, then reduce the heat and simmer, covered, for 15 minutes.

2 Transfer the mixture to a food processor or blender and process until smooth. Return to the rinsed-out saucepan.

3 Reheat the soup, season to taste with salt and pepper, and serve in warmed bowls, swirled with the cream, if using, and garnished with chives.

borscht

ingredients

SERVES 6

1 onion

4 tbsp butter

12 oz/350 g raw beets,
    cut into thin sticks, and
    1 raw beet, grated

1 carrot, cut into thin sticks

3 celery stalks, thinly sliced

2 tomatoes, peeled, seeded,
    and chopped

6^1/$_4$ cups vegetable stock

1 tbsp white wine vinegar

1 tbsp sugar

2 tbsp snipped fresh dill

1 cup shredded white
    cabbage

salt and pepper

^{2}/$_3$ cup sour cream,
    to garnish

crusty bread, to serve

method

1 Slice the onion into rings. Melt the butter in a large heavy-bottom pan. Add the onion and cook over low heat, stirring occasionally, for 3–5 minutes, or until softened. Add the sticks of beet, carrot, celery, and tomatoes and cook, stirring frequently, for 4–5 minutes.

2 Add the stock, vinegar, sugar, and 1 tablespoon of the snipped dill to the pan. Season to taste with salt and pepper. Bring to a boil, reduce the heat, and simmer for 35–40 minutes, or until the vegetables are tender.

3 Stir in the cabbage, cover, and simmer for 10 minutes, then stir in the grated beet, with any juices, and cook for an additional 10 minutes.

4 Ladle the borscht into warmed bowls. Garnish with sour cream and the remaining dill and serve with crusty bread.

beef & vegetable soup

ingredients

SERVES 4

$1/3$ cup pearl barley

5 cups beef stock

1 tsp dried mixed herbs

8 oz/225 g lean sirloin or
    porterhouse steak

1 large carrot, diced

1 leek, shredded

1 onion, chopped

2 celery stalks, sliced

salt and pepper

2 tbsp chopped fresh parsley,
    to garnish

method

1 Place the pearl barley in a large saucepan. Pour over the stock and add the mixed herbs. Bring to a boil, cover, and simmer gently over low heat for 10 minutes.

2 Meanwhile, trim any fat from the beef and cut the meat into thin strips.

3 Skim away any foam that has risen to the top of the stock with a flat ladle.

4 Add the beef, carrot, leek, onion, and celery to the pan. Bring back to a boil, cover, and simmer for about 1 hour, or until the pearl barley, beef, and vegetables are just tender.

5 Skim away any remaining foam that has risen to the top of the soup with a flat ladle. Blot the surface with absorbent paper towels to remove any fat. Season to taste with salt and pepper.

6 Ladle the soup into warmed bowls, garnish with chopped parsley, and serve hot.

mexican-style beef & rice soup

ingredients

SERVES 4

3 tbsp olive oil

1 lb 2 oz/500 g boneless
  braising beef, cut into
  1-inch/2.5-cm pieces

1 onion, finely chopped

1 green bell pepper, cored,
  seeded, and finely
  chopped

1 small fresh red chile, seeded
  and finely chopped

2 garlic cloves, finely chopped

1 carrot, finely chopped

$1/4$ tsp ground coriander

$1/4$ tsp ground cumin

$1/8$ tsp ground cinnamon

$1/4$ tsp dried oregano

1 bay leaf

grated rind of $1/2$ orange

14 oz/400 g canned chopped
  tomatoes

5 cups beef stock

$2/3$ cup red wine

$1/4$ cup long-grain white rice

3 tbsp raisins

$1/2$ oz/15 g semisweet
  chocolate, melted

chopped fresh cilantro,
  to garnish

method

1 Heat half the oil in a large saucepan over medium–high heat. Add the meat in one layer and cook until well browned, turning to color all sides. Using a slotted spoon, transfer the meat to a plate. Drain off the oil and wipe out the pan with paper towels.

2 Heat the remaining oil in the saucepan over medium heat. Add the onion, cover, and cook for about 3 minutes, stirring occasionally, until just softened. Add the bell pepper, chile, garlic, and carrot, and continue cooking, covered, for 3 minutes.

3 Add the coriander, cumin, cinnamon, oregano, bay leaf, and orange rind. Stir in the tomatoes and stock, along with the beef and wine. Bring almost to a boil and when the mixture begins to bubble, reduce the heat to low. Cover and simmer gently, stirring occasionally, for about 1 hour, until the meat is tender.

4 Stir in the rice, raisins, and chocolate and continue cooking, stirring occasionally, for about 30 minutes, until the rice is tender.

5 Ladle into warmed bowls and garnish with cilantro.

spicy lamb soup with chickpeas & zucchini

ingredients

SERVES 4–6

1–2 tbsp olive oil

1 lb/450 g lean boneless
    lamb, such as shoulder
    or neck fillet, trimmed
    of fat and cut into
    1/2-inch/1-cm cubes

1 onion, finely chopped

2–3 garlic cloves, crushed

5 cups water

14 oz/400 g canned chopped
    tomatoes

1 bay leaf

1/2 tsp dried thyme

1/2 tsp dried oregano

1/8 tsp ground cinnamon

1/2 tsp ground cumin

1/4 tsp ground turmeric

1 tsp harissa, or to taste

14 oz/400 g canned chickpeas,
    rinsed and drained

1 carrot, diced

1 potato, diced

1 zucchini, quartered
    lengthwise and sliced

2/3 cup fresh or defrosted
    frozen green peas

fresh mint sprigs, to garnish

method

1 Heat 1 tablespoon of the oil in a large saucepan or cast-iron casserole over a medium–high heat. Add the lamb, in batches if necessary to avoid crowding the pan, and cook until evenly browned on all sides, adding a little more oil if needed. Remove the meat with a slotted spoon when browned.

2 Reduce the heat and add the onion and garlic to the pan. Cook, stirring frequently, for 1–2 minutes.

3 Add the water and return all the meat to the pan. Bring just to a boil and skim off any foam that rises to the surface. Reduce the heat and stir in the tomatoes, bay leaf, thyme, oregano, cinnamon, cumin, turmeric, and harissa. Simmer for about 1 hour, or until the meat is very tender. Discard the bay leaf.

4 Stir in the chickpeas, carrot, and potato and simmer for 15 minutes. Add the zucchini and peas and continue simmering for 15–20 minutes, or until all the vegetables are tender.

5 Adjust the seasoning, adding more harissa, if desired. Ladle the soup into warmed bowls and garnish with mint sprigs.

hearty winter broth

ingredients

SERVES 6–8

1 lb 9 oz/700 g neck of lamb

7¼ cups water

generous 1 cup pearl barley

2 onions, chopped

1 garlic clove, finely chopped

3 small turnips, cut into small
   dice

3 carrots, peeled and thinly
   sliced

2 celery stalks, sliced

2 leeks, sliced

salt and pepper

2 tbsp chopped fresh parsley,
   to garnish

method

1 Cut the meat into small pieces, removing as much fat as possible. Put into a large pan and cover with the water. Bring to a boil over medium heat and skim off any foam that forms.

2 Add the pearl barley, reduce the heat, and cook gently, covered, for 1 hour.

3 Add the prepared vegetables and season well with salt and pepper. Continue to cook for an additional hour. Remove from the heat and let cool slightly.

4 Remove the meat from the pan using a slotted spoon and strip the meat from the bones. Discard the bones and any fat or gristle. Put the meat back into the pan and let cool thoroughly, then cover and refrigerate overnight.

5 Scrape the solidified fat off the surface of the soup. Reheat, season to taste with salt and pepper, and serve piping hot, garnished with the parsley.

pork chili soup

ingredients

SERVES 4

2 tsp olive oil

1 lb 2 oz/500 g lean ground
   pork

1 onion, finely chopped

1 celery stalk, finely chopped

1 red or green bell pepper,
   cored, seeded, and finely
   chopped

2–3 garlic cloves, finely
   chopped

14 oz/400 g canned chopped
   tomatoes

3 tbsp tomato paste

2 cups chicken or meat stock

$1/8$ tsp ground coriander

$1/8$ tsp ground cumin

$1/4$ tsp dried oregano

1 tsp mild chili powder,
   or to taste

salt and pepper

chopped fresh cilantro,
   to garnish

sour cream, to serve

method

1 Heat the oil in a large saucepan over medium–high heat. Add the pork, season to taste with salt and pepper, and cook until no longer pink, stirring frequently. Reduce the heat to medium and add the onion, celery, bell pepper, and garlic. Cover and continue cooking for 5 minutes, stirring occasionally, until the onion is softened.

2 Add the tomatoes, tomato paste, and stock. Add the coriander, cumin, oregano, and chili powder. Stir the ingredients to combine well.

3 Bring just to a boil, reduce the heat to low, cover, and simmer for 30–40 minutes, until all the vegetables are very tender. Taste and adjust the seasoning, adding more chili powder if you like it hotter.

4 Ladle the chili into warmed bowls and sprinkle with chopped cilantro. Pass the sour cream separately, or top each serving with a spoonful.

pork & vegetable broth

ingredients

SERVES 4

1 tbsp chili oil

1 garlic clove, chopped

3 scallions, sliced

1 red bell pepper, seeded and
   finely sliced

2 tbsp cornstarch

4 cups vegetable stock

1 tbsp soy sauce

2 tbsp rice wine or dry sherry

5$\frac{1}{2}$ oz/150 g pork tenderloin,
   sliced

1 tbsp finely chopped
   lemongrass

1 small fresh red chile,
   seeded and finely
   chopped

1 tbsp grated fresh ginger

4 oz/115 g fine egg noodles

7 oz/200 g canned water
   chestnuts, drained
   and sliced

salt and pepper

method

1 Heat the oil in a large pan. Add the garlic and scallions and cook over medium heat, stirring, for 3 minutes, until slightly softened. Add the bell pepper and cook for an additional 5 minutes, stirring.

2 In a bowl, mix the cornstarch with enough of the stock to make a smooth paste and stir it into the pan. Cook, stirring, for 2 minutes. Stir in the remaining stock, the soy sauce, and rice wine, then add the pork, lemongrass, chile, and ginger. Season to taste with salt and pepper. Bring to a boil, then lower the heat and simmer for 25 minutes.

3 Bring a separate pan of water to a boil, add the noodles, and cook for 3 minutes. Remove from the heat, drain, then add the noodles to the soup along with the water chestnuts. Cook for another 2 minutes, then remove from the heat and ladle into serving bowls.

bacon & lentil soup

ingredients

SERVES 4

1 lb/450 g thick, rindless
   smoked bacon strips, diced

1 onion, chopped

2 carrots, sliced

2 celery stalks, chopped

1 turnip, chopped

1 large potato, chopped

generous 2^1/$_4$ cups Puy lentils

1 bouquet garni

4 cups water or chicken stock

salt and pepper

method

1 Heat a large heavy-bottom pan or flameproof casserole. Add the bacon and cook over medium heat, stirring, for 4–5 minutes, or until the fat runs. Add the onion, carrots, celery, turnip, and potato and cook, stirring frequently, for 5 minutes.

2 Add the lentils and bouquet garni and pour in the water. Bring to a boil, reduce the heat, and simmer for 1 hour, or until the lentils are tender.

3 Remove and discard the bouquet garni and season the soup to taste with pepper, and with salt if necessary. Ladle into warmed soup bowls and serve.

chicken & leek soup

ingredients

SERVES 6–8

2 tbsp vegetable oil or olive oil

2 onions, coarsely chopped

2 carrots, coarsely chopped

5 leeks, 2 coarsely chopped,
   3 thinly sliced

1 chicken, weighing
   3 lb/1.3 kg

2 bay leaves

6 prunes, sliced

salt and pepper

fresh parsley sprigs,
   to garnish

method

1 Heat the oil in a large pan over medium heat, add the onions, carrots, and coarsely chopped leeks, and cook for 3–4 minutes, until just golden brown. Wipe the chicken inside and out and remove and discard any excess skin and fat.

2 Put the chicken into the pan with the cooked vegetables and add the bay leaves. Pour in enough cold water to just cover and season well with salt and pepper. Bring to a boil, then reduce the heat, cover, and simmer for 1–1 1/2 hours. Skim off any foam that forms from time to time.

3 Remove the chicken from the stock, remove and discard the skin, then remove all the meat. Cut the meat into neat pieces.

4 Strain the stock through a colander, discard the vegetables and bay leaves, and return to the rinsed-out pan. Expect to have 4–5 cups of stock. If you have time, it is a good idea to let the stock cool so that the fat solidifies and can be removed. If not, blot the fat off the surface with paper towels.

5 Heat the stock to simmering point, add the sliced leeks and prunes to the pan, and heat for about 1 minute. Return the chicken to the pan and heat through. Serve immediately in warmed deep dishes, garnished with parsley sprigs.

chicken-noodle soup

ingredients

SERVES 4–6

2 skinless chicken breasts

8 cups water

1 onion, unpeeled, cut in half

1 large garlic clove, cut in half

$^1/_2$-inch/1-cm piece fresh
   ginger, peeled and sliced

4 black peppercorns, lightly
   crushed

4 cloves

2 star anise

1 carrot, peeled

1 celery stalk, chopped

$3^1/_2$ oz/100 g baby corn, cut
   in half lengthwise and
   chopped

2 scallions, finely shredded

4 oz/115 g dried rice
   vermicelli noodles

salt and pepper

method

1 Put the chicken breasts and water in a pan over high heat and bring to a boil. Reduce the heat to its lowest setting and let simmer, skimming the surface until no more foam rises.

2 Add the onion, garlic, ginger, peppercorns, cloves, star anise, and a pinch of salt and continue to simmer for 20 minutes, or until the chicken is tender and cooked through.

3 Meanwhile, grate the carrot along its length on the coarse side of a grater so you get long, thin strips.

4 Strain the chicken, reserving about 5 cups stock, but discarding any flavoring solids. (At this point you can let the stock cool and refrigerate overnight, so any fat solidifies and can be lifted off and discarded.) Return the stock to the rinsed-out pan with the carrot, celery, baby corn, and scallions and bring to a boil. Boil until the baby corn are almost tender, then add the noodles and continue boiling for 2 minutes.

5 Meanwhile, chop the chicken, add to the pan, and continue cooking for an additional minute, until the chicken is reheated and the noodles are soft. Season to taste with salt and pepper, then divide among warmed bowls to serve.

chicken & rice soup

ingredients

SERVES 4

6$^1/_4$ cups chicken stock

2 small carrots, very thinly
   sliced

1 celery stalk, finely diced

1 baby leek, halved lengthwise
   and thinly sliced

$^3/_4$ cup petit pois, defrosted
   if frozen

1 cup cooked rice

5$^1/_2$ oz/150 g cooked chicken,
   sliced

2 tsp chopped fresh tarragon

1 tbsp chopped fresh parsley,
   plus extra sprigs to garnish

salt and pepper

method

1 Put the stock in a large saucepan and add the carrots, celery, and leek. Bring to a boil, reduce the heat to low, and simmer gently, partially covered, for 10 minutes.

2 Stir in the petit pois, rice, and chicken and continue cooking for an additional 10–15 minutes, or until the vegetables are tender.

3 Add the chopped tarragon and parsley, then taste and adjust the seasoning, adding salt and pepper as needed.

4 Ladle the soup into warmed bowls, garnish with parsley sprigs, and serve.

chicken gumbo soup

ingredients

SERVES 6

2 tbsp olive oil

4 tbsp all-purpose flour

1 onion, finely chopped

1 small green bell pepper,
    seeded and finely
    chopped

1 celery stalk, finely chopped

5 cups chicken stock

14 oz/400 g canned chopped
    tomatoes

3 garlic cloves, finely
    chopped or crushed

4½ oz/125 g okra, stems
    removed, cut into
    ¼ inch/5 mm thick slices

4 tbsp white rice

7 oz/200 g cooked chicken,
    cubed

4 oz/115 g cooked garlic
    sausage, sliced or cubed

salt and pepper

method

1 Heat the oil in a large heavy-bottom saucepan over low–medium heat and stir in the flour. Cook for about 15 minutes, stirring occasionally, until the mixture is a rich golden brown.

2 Add the onion, bell pepper, and celery and continue cooking for about 10 minutes, until the onion softens.

3 Slowly pour in the stock and bring to a boil, stirring well and scraping the bottom of the pan to mix in the flour. Remove the pan from the heat.

4 Add the tomatoes and garlic. Return to the heat, stir in the okra and rice, and season to taste with salt and pepper. Bring to a boil, then reduce the heat, cover, and simmer for 20 minutes, or until the okra is tender.

5 Add the chicken and sausage and continue simmering for about 10 minutes. Taste and adjust the seasoning, if necessary, and ladle into warmed bowls to serve.

turkey & lentil soup

ingredients

SERVES 4

1 tbsp olive oil

1 garlic clove, chopped

1 large onion, chopped

7 oz/200 g button
    mushrooms, sliced

1 red bell pepper, seeded
    and chopped

6 tomatoes, skinned, seeded,
    and chopped

generous 4 cups chicken stock

$^2/_3$ cup red wine

1 cup cauliflower florets

1 carrot, peeled and chopped

1 cup red lentils

12 oz/350 g cooked turkey
    meat, chopped

1 zucchini, trimmed and
    chopped

1 tbsp shredded fresh basil,
    plus extra leaves
    to garnish

salt and pepper

thick slices of crusty bread,
    to serve

method

1 Heat the oil in a large pan. Add the garlic and onion and cook over medium heat, stirring, for 3 minutes, until slightly softened.

2 Add the mushrooms, bell pepper, and tomatoes, and cook for an additional 5 minutes, stirring.

3 Pour in the stock and red wine, then add the cauliflower, carrot, and red lentils. Season to taste with salt and pepper. Bring to a boil, then lower the heat and simmer for 25 minutes, until the vegetables are tender and cooked through.

4 Add the turkey and zucchini to the pan and cook for 10 minutes. Stir in the shredded basil and cook for an additional 5 minutes, then remove from the heat and ladle into serving bowls. Garnish with fresh basil leaves and serve with crusty bread.

bouillabaisse

ingredients

SERVES 4

7 oz/200 g live mussels

scant 1/2 cup olive oil

3 garlic cloves, chopped

2 onions, chopped

2 tomatoes, seeded and
    chopped

generous 2 3/4 cups fish stock

1 3/4 cups white wine

1 bay leaf

pinch of saffron threads

2 tbsp chopped fresh basil

2 tbsp chopped fresh parsley

9 oz/250 g snapper or
    monkfish fillets

9 oz/250 g whitefish fillets,
    skinned

7 oz/200 g shrimp, peeled
    and deveined

3 1/2 oz/100 g scallops

salt and pepper

fresh baguettes, to serve

method

1 Soak the mussels in lightly salted water for 10 minutes. Scrub the shells under cold running water and pull off any beards. Discard any with broken shells. Tap the remaining mussels and discard any that refuse to close. Put the rest into a large pan with a little water, bring to a boil, and cook over high heat for 4 minutes. Transfer the cooked mussels to a bowl, discarding any that remain closed, and reserve. Wipe out the pan with paper towels.

2 Heat the oil in the pan over medium heat. Add the garlic and onions and cook, stirring, for 3 minutes. Stir in the tomatoes, stock, wine, bay leaf, saffron, and herbs. Bring to a boil, reduce the heat, cover, and simmer for 30 minutes.

3 When the tomato mixture is cooked, rinse the fish, pat dry, and cut into chunks. Add to the pan and simmer for 5 minutes. Add the reserved mussels, the shrimp, and scallops, and season to taste with salt and pepper. Cook for 3 minutes, until the fish is cooked through.

4 Remove from the heat, discard the bay leaf, and ladle into serving bowls. Serve with fresh baguettes.

laksa

ingredients

SERVES 4

1 tbsp corn oil

2–3 garlic cloves, cut into thin
slivers

1–2 fresh red Thai chiles,
seeded and sliced

2 lemongrass stalks, outer
leaves removed, chopped

1-inch/2.5-cm piece fresh
ginger, grated

5 cups fish stock or vegetable
stock

12 oz/350 g large raw shrimp,
peeled and deveined

4 oz/115 g shiitake
mushrooms, sliced

1 large carrot, grated

2 oz/55 g dried egg noodles
(optional)

1–2 tsp Thai fish sauce

1 tbsp chopped fresh cilantro

method

1 Heat the oil in a large pan over medium
heat, add the garlic, chiles, lemongrass,
and ginger, and cook for 5 minutes, stirring
frequently. Add the stock and bring to a boil,
then reduce the heat and let simmer for
5 minutes.

2 Stir in the shrimp, mushrooms, and carrot.
If using the egg noodles, break into short
lengths, add to the pan, and let simmer for an
additional 5 minutes, or until the shrimp have
turned pink and the noodles are tender.

3 Stir in the Thai fish sauce and cilantro
and heat through for an additional minute
before serving.

seafood chowder

ingredients

SERVES 6

2 lb 4 oz/1 kg live mussels,
   scrubbed and debearded

4 tbsp all-purpose flour

6$\frac{1}{4}$ cups fish stock

1 tbsp butter

1 large onion, finely chopped

12 oz/350 g skinless whitefish
   fillets, such as cod or sole

7 oz/200 g cooked or raw
   peeled shrimp

1$\frac{1}{4}$ cups heavy cream

salt and pepper

snipped fresh dill, to garnish

method

1 Discard any mussels with broken shells and any that refuse to close when tapped. Rinse the remaining mussels under cold running water and place in a large heavy-bottom saucepan. Cover tightly and cook over high heat for about 4 minutes, or until the mussels open, shaking the pan occasionally. Discard any that remain closed. When cool enough to handle, remove the mussels from the shells, adding any additional juices to the cooking liquid. Strain the cooking liquid and reserve.

2 Put the flour in a bowl and slowly whisk in enough of the stock to make a thick paste. Whisk in a little more stock to make a smooth liquid.

3 Melt the butter in a heavy-bottom saucepan over low–medium heat. Add the onion, cover, and cook for about 5 minutes, stirring frequently, until it softens. Add the remaining stock and bring to a boil. Slowly whisk in the flour mixture and bring back to a boil, whisking constantly. Add the mussel cooking liquid. Season to taste with salt, if needed, and pepper. Reduce the heat and simmer, partially covered, for 15 minutes.

4 Add the fish and the reserved mussels and continue simmering, stirring occasionally, for about 5 minutes, or until the fish is cooked.

5 Stir in the shrimp and cream. Simmer for a few minutes longer to heat through. Ladle into warmed bowls, garnish with dill, and serve.

clam & corn chowder

ingredients

SERVES 4

4 tsp butter

1 large onion, finely chopped

1 small carrot, finely diced

3 tbsp all-purpose flour

1¼ cups fish stock

¾ cup water

1 lb/450 g potatoes, diced

1 cup cooked or defrosted
   frozen corn kernels

2 cups whole milk

10 oz/280 g canned clams,
   drained and rinsed

salt and pepper

chopped fresh parsley,
   to garnish

method

1 Melt the butter in a large saucepan over a low–medium heat. Add the onion and carrot and cook for 3–4 minutes, stirring frequently, until the onion is softened. Stir in the flour and continue cooking for 2 minutes.

2 Slowly add about half the stock and stir well, scraping the bottom of the pan to mix in the flour. Pour in the remaining stock and the water and bring just to a boil, stirring.

3 Add the potatoes, corn, and milk and stir to combine. Reduce the heat and simmer gently, partially covered, for about 20 minutes, stirring occasionally, until all the vegetables are tender.

4 Chop the clams, if large. Stir in the clams and continue cooking for about 5 minutes, until heated through. Taste and adjust the seasoning, adding salt and pepper if needed.

5 Ladle the soup into bowls and sprinkle with parsley.

meat

Coming home on a cold day to the enticing aroma of a gently simmering stew is one of life's great pleasures, superseded only by sitting down to eat it. Whether succulent beef braised in wine and herbs, a fragrant stew of tender lamb and spices, or a heart-warming mixture of pork and colorful vegetables, slow-cooked one-pot dishes are full of flavor and substantial enough to satisfy the heartiest appetite. Not only are these great family meals, but they are also perfect for easy entertaining. The same, of course, is true of pot roasts, which have all the flavor and variety of oven-roasted meat, but are far less trouble to cook and much less time-consuming to clear up. What's more, you can guarantee that a pot roast will be moist and tender.

There isn't always time to cook a casserole and stews may be too heavy for summer suppers, but there are still easy one-pot dishes for family meals. You can make a fabulous Thai curry in less than 15 minutes or a classic creamy stroganoff in only half an hour. With recipes inspired by countries across the globe, you are sure to find a whole range of delicious one-pot dishes destined to become family favorites.

beef pot roast with potatoes & dill

ingredients

SERVES 6

2 1/2 tbsp all-purpose flour

1 tsp salt

1/4 tsp pepper

1 rolled brisket joint, weighing
    3 lb 8 oz/1.6 kg

2 tbsp vegetable oil

2 tbsp butter

1 onion, finely chopped

2 celery stalks, diced

2 carrots, peeled and diced

1 tsp dill seed

1 tsp dried thyme or oregano

1 1/2 cups red wine

2/3–1 cup beef stock

4–5 potatoes, cut into large
    chunks and boiled until
    just tender

2 tbsp chopped fresh dill,
    to serve

method

1 Preheat the oven to 275°F/140°C. Mix 2 tablespoons of the flour with the salt and pepper in a shallow dish. Dip the meat to coat. Heat the oil in a flameproof casserole and brown the meat all over. Transfer to a plate.

2 Add half the butter to the casserole and cook the onion, celery, carrots, dill seed, and thyme for 5 minutes. Return the meat and juices to the casserole.

3 Pour in the wine and enough stock to reach one-third of the way up the meat. Bring to a boil, cover, and cook in the oven for 2 hours, turning the meat every 30 minutes. Add the potatoes to the casserole with a little more stock, if necessary, and return to the oven for an additional hour.

4 When ready, transfer the meat and potatoes to a warmed serving dish. Strain the cooking liquid to remove any solids, then return the liquid to the casserole.

5 Mix the remaining butter and flour to a paste. Bring the cooking liquid to a boil. Whisk in small pieces of the flour-and-butter paste, whisking constantly until the sauce is smooth. Pour the sauce over the meat and potatoes. Sprinkle with the fresh dill to serve.

beef in beer with herb dumplings

ingredients

SERVES 6

2 tbsp corn oil

2 large onions, thinly sliced

8 carrots, sliced

4 tbsp all-purpose flour

2 lb 12 oz/1.25 kg braising
    beef, cut into cubes

generous 1³/4 cups stout

2 tsp brown sugar

2 bay leaves

1 tbsp chopped fresh thyme

salt and pepper

herb dumplings

generous ³/4 cup self-rising
    flour

pinch of salt

¹/2 cup shredded suet

2 tbsp chopped fresh parsley,
    plus extra to garnish

about 4 tbsp water

method

1 Preheat the oven to 325°F/160°C. Heat the oil in a flameproof casserole. Add the onions and carrots and cook over low heat, stirring occasionally, for 5 minutes, or until the onions are softened. Meanwhile, place the flour in a plastic bag and season to taste with salt and pepper. Add the braising beef to the bag, tie the top, and shake well to coat. Do this in batches, if necessary.

2 Remove the vegetables from the casserole with a slotted spoon and reserve. Add the braising beef to the casserole, in batches, and cook, stirring frequently, until browned all over. Return all the meat and the vegetables to the casserole and sprinkle in any remaining seasoned flour. Pour in the stout and add the sugar, bay leaves, and thyme. Bring to a boil, cover, and transfer to the preheated oven to bake for 1³/4 hours.

3 To make the herb dumplings, sift the flour and salt into a bowl. Stir in the suet and parsley and add enough of the water to make a soft dough. Shape into small balls between the palms of your hands. Add to the casserole and return to the oven for 30 minutes.

4 Remove and discard the bay leaves and serve, sprinkled with parsley.

daube of beef

ingredients

SERVES 6

$1^1/2$ cups dry white wine

2 tbsp brandy

1 tbsp white wine vinegar

4 shallots, sliced

4 carrots, sliced

1 garlic clove, finely chopped

6 black peppercorns

4 fresh thyme sprigs

1 fresh rosemary sprig

2 fresh parsley sprigs,
    plus extra to garnish

1 bay leaf

1 lb 10 oz/750 g beef top
    round, cut into 1-inch/
    2.5-cm cubes

1–2 tbsp olive oil

1 lb 12 oz/800 g canned
    chopped tomatoes

8 oz/225 g portobello
    mushrooms, sliced

strip of finely pared orange
    rind

2 oz/55 g prosciutto, cut into
    strips

12 black olives

salt

method

1 Combine the wine, brandy, vinegar, shallots, carrots, garlic, peppercorns, thyme, rosemary, parsley, and bay leaf and season to taste with salt. Add the beef, stirring to coat, then cover with plastic wrap and let marinate in the refrigerator for 8 hours, or overnight.

2 Preheat the oven to 300°F/150°C. Drain the beef, reserving the marinade, and pat dry on paper towels. Heat 1 tablespoon of the oil in a large flameproof casserole. Add the beef cubes in batches and cook over medium heat, stirring, for 3–4 minutes, or until browned, adding more oil if necessary. Using a slotted spoon, transfer each batch to a plate.

3 Return all of the beef to the casserole and add the tomatoes and their juices, mushrooms, and orange rind. Strain the reserved marinade into the casserole. Bring to a boil, cover, and cook in the preheated oven for $2^1/2$ hours.

4 Remove the casserole from the oven, add the prosciutto and olives, and return it to the oven to cook for an additional 30 minutes, or until the beef is very tender. Discard the orange rind and serve straight from the casserole, garnished with parsley sprigs.

beef goulash

ingredients

SERVES 4

2 tbsp vegetable oil

1 large onion, chopped

1 garlic clove, crushed

1 lb 10 oz/750 g lean braising
   beef, cut into chunks

2 tbsp paprika

15 oz/425 g canned chopped
   tomatoes

2 tbsp tomato paste

1 large red bell pepper,
   seeded and chopped

6 oz/175 g button
   mushrooms, sliced

$2^1/2$ cups beef stock

1 tbsp cornstarch

1 tbsp water

salt and pepper

chopped fresh parsley,
   to garnish

freshly cooked long-grain and
   wild rice, to serve

method

1 Heat the oil in a large pan and cook the onion and garlic for 3–4 minutes.

2 Add the beef and cook over high heat for 3 minutes, until browned all over. Add the paprika and stir well, then add the tomatoes, tomato paste, bell pepper, and mushrooms. Cook for 2 minutes, stirring frequently.

3 Pour in the beef stock. Bring to a boil, then reduce the heat. Cover and simmer for $1^1/2$–2 hours, until the meat is tender.

4 Blend the cornstarch with the water, then add to the pan, stirring until thickened and smooth. Cook for 1 minute, then season to taste with salt and pepper.

5 Transfer the beef goulash to a warmed serving dish, garnish with chopped fresh parsley, and serve with rice.

chili con carne

ingredients

SERVES 4

1 lb 10 oz/750 g lean braising
  beef
2 tbsp vegetable oil
1 large onion, sliced
2–4 garlic cloves, crushed
1 tbsp all-purpose flour
generous 1¾ cups tomato
  juice
14 oz/400 g canned chopped
  tomatoes
1–2 tbsp sweet chili sauce
1 tsp ground cumin
15 oz/425 g canned red
  kidney beans, drained
  and rinsed
½ tsp dried oregano
1–2 tbsp chopped fresh
  parsley, plus extra sprigs
  to garnish
salt and pepper
freshly cooked rice and
  tortillas, to serve

method

1 Preheat the oven to 325°F/160°C. Using a sharp knife, cut the beef into ¾-inch/2-cm cubes. Heat the oil in a large flameproof casserole and cook the beef over medium heat until well sealed on all sides. Remove the beef from the casserole with a slotted spoon and set aside until required.

2 Add the onion and garlic to the casserole and cook until lightly browned; then stir in the flour and cook for 1–2 minutes.

3 Stir in the tomato juice and tomatoes and bring to a boil. Return the beef to the casserole and add the chili sauce, cumin, and salt and pepper to taste. Cover and cook in the preheated oven for 1½ hours, or until the beef is almost tender.

4 Stir in the kidney beans, oregano, and chopped parsley, and adjust the seasoning to taste, if necessary. Cover the casserole and return to the oven for 45 minutes. Transfer to 4 large warmed serving plates, garnish with parsley sprigs, and serve immediately with freshly cooked rice and tortillas.

beef stroganoff

ingredients

SERVES 4

$^1/_2$ oz/15 g dried porcini
   mushrooms

12 oz/350 g beef tenderloin

2 tbsp olive oil

4 shallots, sliced

6 oz/175 g cremini
   mushrooms

$^1/_2$ tsp Dijon mustard

5 tbsp heavy cream

salt and pepper

freshly cooked pasta, to serve

fresh chives, to garnish

method

1 Place the dried porcini mushrooms in a bowl and cover with hot water. Let soak for 20 minutes. Meanwhile, cut the beef against the grain into $^1/_4$ inch/5 mm thick slices, then into $^1/_2$ inch/1 cm long strips, and reserve.

2 Drain the mushrooms, reserving the soaking liquid, and chop. Strain the soaking liquid through a fine-mesh strainer or coffee filter and reserve.

3 Heat half the oil in a large skillet. Add the shallots and cook over low heat, stirring occasionally, for 5 minutes, or until softened. Add the dried mushrooms, reserved soaking water, and whole cremini mushrooms and cook, stirring frequently, for 10 minutes, or until almost all of the liquid has evaporated, then transfer the mixture to a plate.

4 Heat the remaining oil in the skillet, add the beef, and cook, stirring frequently, for 4 minutes, or until browned all over. You may need to do this in batches. Return the mushroom mixture to the skillet and season to taste with salt and pepper.

5 Place the mustard and cream in a small bowl and stir to mix, then fold into the mixture. Heat through gently, then serve with freshly cooked pasta and garnish with chives.

beef & vegetable stew with corn

ingredients

SERVES 4

1 lb/450 g braising beef

1^1/$_2$ tbsp all-purpose flour

1 tsp hot paprika

1–1^1/$_2$ tsp chili powder

1 tsp ground ginger

2 tbsp olive oil

1 large onion, cut into chunks

3 garlic cloves, sliced

2 celery stalks, sliced

4 carrots, chopped

1^1/$_4$ cups lager

1^1/$_4$ cups beef stock

3 potatoes, chopped

1 red bell pepper, seeded
    and chopped

2 corn cobs, halved

1 small tomato, cut into
    quarters

1 cup shelled fresh or frozen
    peas

1 tbsp chopped fresh cilantro

salt and pepper

method

1 Trim any fat or gristle from the beef and cut into 1-inch/2.5-cm chunks. Mix the flour and spices together. Toss the beef in the spiced flour until well coated.

2 Heat the oil in a large heavy-bottom pan and cook the onion, garlic, and celery, stirring frequently, for 5 minutes, or until softened. Add the beef and cook over high heat, stirring frequently, for 3 minutes, or until browned on all sides and sealed.

3 Add the carrots, then remove from the heat. Gradually stir in the lager and stock, then return to the heat and bring to a boil, stirring. Reduce the heat, then cover and simmer, stirring occasionally, for 1^1/$_2$ hours.

4 Add the potatoes to the pan and simmer for an additional 15 minutes. Add the bell pepper and corn cobs and simmer for 15 minutes, then add the tomato and peas and simmer for an additional 10 minutes, or until the beef and vegetables are tender. Season to taste with salt and pepper, then stir in the cilantro and serve.

beef pepper pot stew

ingredients

SERVES 4

1 lb/450 g braising beef

1^1/$_2$ tbsp all-purpose flour

2 tbsp olive oil

1 red onion, chopped

3–4 garlic cloves, crushed

1 fresh green chile, seeded
    and chopped

3 celery stalks, sliced

4 whole cloves

1 tsp ground allspice

1–2 tsp hot pepper sauce,
    or to taste

2^1/$_2$ cups beef stock

^{1}/$_2$ large acorn squash,
    seeded, peeled, and
    cut into chunks

1 large red bell pepper,
    seeded and chopped

4 tomatoes, coarsely chopped

4 oz/115 g okra, trimmed and
    halved

freshly cooked rice, to serve

method

1 Trim any fat or gristle from the beef and cut into 1-inch/2.5-cm chunks. Toss the beef in the flour until well coated and reserve any remaining flour.

2 Heat the oil in a large heavy-bottom pan and cook the onion, garlic, chile, and celery with the cloves and allspice, stirring frequently, for 5 minutes, or until softened. Add the beef and cook over high heat, stirring frequently, for 3 minutes, or until browned on all sides and sealed. Sprinkle in the reserved flour and cook, stirring constantly, for 2 minutes, then remove from the heat.

3 Add the hot pepper sauce and gradually stir in the stock, then return to the heat and bring to a boil, stirring. Reduce the heat, then cover and simmer, stirring occasionally, for 1^1/$_2$ hours.

4 Add the squash and bell pepper to the pan and simmer for an additional 15 minutes. Add the tomatoes and okra and simmer for an additional 15 minutes, or until the beef is tender. Serve with cooked rice.

beef chop suey

ingredients

SERVES 4

1 lb/450 g porterhouse steak, thinly sliced

2 tbsp vegetable oil or peanut oil

1 onion, thinly sliced

2 celery stalks, thinly sliced diagonally

1 head of broccoli, cut into small florets, blanched

2 cups snow peas, sliced in half lengthwise

$^1/_2$ cup canned bamboo shoots, rinsed and julienned

8 water chestnuts, thinly sliced

4 cups thinly sliced button mushrooms

1 tbsp oyster sauce

1 tsp salt

marinade

1 tbsp Chinese rice wine

pinch of white pepper

pinch of salt

1 tbsp light soy sauce

$^1/_2$ tsp sesame oil

method

1 Combine all the marinade ingredients in a bowl and marinate the beef for at least 20 minutes.

2 In a preheated wok or deep pan, heat 1 tablespoon of the oil and stir-fry the beef until the color has changed. Remove and set aside. Wipe out the wok or pan with paper towels.

3 In the clean wok or deep pan, heat the remaining oil and stir-fry the onion for 1 minute. Add the celery and broccoli and cook for 2 minutes. Add the snow peas, bamboo shoots, water chestnuts, and mushrooms and cook for 1 minute. Add the beef, then season with the oyster sauce and salt and serve.

caramelized lamb shanks

ingredients

SERVES 4

4 tbsp honey

1 tbsp vegetable oil

1 tsp dried thyme or oregano

2 tsp pepper

$1/2$ tsp salt

4 lamb shanks, about
14 oz/400 g each

$1^1/2$–2 cups stock

1 head garlic, unpeeled,
sliced in half across
the center

1 onion, quartered

1 parsnip, quartered
lengthwise

4 small new potatoes, halved
lengthwise

4 small carrots

method

1 Preheat the oven to 350°F/180°C. Mix together the honey, oil, thyme, pepper, and salt, and rub all over the lamb shanks. Put the lamb shanks in a roasting pan with $3/4$ cup of the stock, the garlic, and onion.

2 Cook in the preheated oven for 1 hour, turning the lamb after 30 minutes. Turn again, and add the parsnip, potatoes, carrots, and $2/3$ cup of the remaining stock. Cook for an additional 30 minutes and turn the lamb again. Add a little more stock, if necessary, then cook for an additional 15 minutes.

3 Using a slotted spoon, transfer the meat and vegetables to a warmed serving dish. Using paper towels, remove any excess fat from the surface of the liquid in the pan. Place the pan over medium heat and stir for a few seconds, until the liquid is syrupy. Pour over the meat and vegetables and serve immediately.

slow-cooked lamb with celery root

ingredients

SERVES 4

1 leg of lamb, on the bone,
  weighing 5 lb 8 oz/2.5 kg
2 whole heads garlic
grated rind of 2 lemons and
  juice of 1
2 tbsp finely chopped fresh
  rosemary
3 tbsp extra virgin olive oil
3 shallots, coarsely chopped
1¹/₂ cups dry white wine
2 lb 4 oz/1 kg celery root,
  peeled and cut into
  large chunks
salt and pepper

method

1 Score gently through the fat on the lamb in a diamond pattern. Put in a nonmetallic dish. Separate the heads of garlic into cloves. Peel and crush 4 of the garlic cloves and reserve the remainder. Mix together the crushed garlic, lemon rind and juice, and rosemary. Season well with salt and pepper, then stir in the oil. Rub the mixture all over the meat. Cover and let marinate in the refrigerator for several hours, or overnight.

2 Preheat the oven to 425°F/220°C. Transfer the lamb to a roasting pan and pour over the marinade. Roast in the preheated oven for 20 minutes.

3 Reduce the oven temperature to 375°F/190°C. Add the reserved whole garlic cloves, shallots, wine, cover with foil, and roast for an additional 1 hour 40 minutes, basting occasionally. Remove the foil, then add the celery root and turn to coat in the pan juices. Cook with the lamb for an additional 20 minutes.

4 Remove the roasting pan from the oven, then lift out the lamb and keep warm. Return the roasting pan to the oven, then roast for an additional 10–15 minutes, or until golden.

5 Carve the lamb and serve with the celery root, drizzling over the pan juices.

lamb & potato stew

ingredients

SERVES 4

4 tbsp all-purpose flour

3 lb/1.3 kg middle neck of
   lamb, trimmed of visible fat

3 large onions, chopped

3 carrots, sliced

1 lb/450 g potatoes, cut into
   quarters

$^1/_2$ tsp dried thyme

scant 3$^1/_2$ cups beef stock

salt and pepper

2 tbsp chopped fresh parsley,
   to garnish

method

1 Preheat the oven to 325°F/160°C. Spread the flour on a plate and season to taste with salt and pepper. Roll the pieces of lamb in the flour to coat, shaking off any excess, and arrange in the bottom of a casserole.

2 Layer the onions, carrots, and potatoes on top of the lamb.

3 Sprinkle in the thyme and pour in the stock, then cover and cook in the preheated oven for 2$^1/_2$ hours. Garnish with the chopped parsley and serve straight from the casserole.

lamb stew with chickpeas

ingredients

SERVES 4-6

6 tbsp olive oil

8 oz/225 g chorizo sausage, cut into $^1/_4$ inch/5 mm thick slices, casings removed

2 large onions, chopped

6 large garlic cloves, crushed

2 lb/900 g boned leg of lamb, cut into 2-inch/5-cm chunks

scant $1^1/_4$ cups lamb stock or water

$^1/_2$ cup red wine, such as Rioja or Tempranillo

2 tbsp sherry vinegar

1 lb 12 oz/800 g canned chopped tomatoes

4 fresh thyme sprigs, plus extra to garnish

2 bay leaves, to garnish

$^1/_2$ tsp sweet Spanish paprika

1 lb 12 oz/800 g canned chickpeas, rinsed and drained

salt and pepper

method

1 Preheat the oven to 325°F/160°C. Heat 4 tablespoons of the oil in a large heavy-bottom flameproof casserole over medium–high heat. Reduce the heat, add the chorizo, and cook for 1 minute; set aside. Add the onions to the casserole and cook for 2 minutes, then add the garlic and continue cooking for 3 minutes, or until the onions are softened but not browned. Remove from the casserole and set aside.

2 Heat the remaining 2 tablespoons of oil in the casserole. Add the lamb cubes in a single layer without overcrowding the casserole, and cook until browned on each side, working in batches if necessary.

3 Return the onion mixture to the casserole with all the lamb. Stir in the stock, wine, vinegar, tomatoes with their juices, and salt and pepper to taste. Bring to a boil, scraping any sediments from the bottom of the casserole. Reduce the heat and stir in the thyme, bay leaves, and paprika.

4 Transfer to the preheated oven and cook, covered, for 40–45 minutes, until the lamb is tender. Stir in the chickpeas and return to the oven, uncovered, for 10 minutes, or until they are heated through and the juices are reduced.

5 Taste and adjust the seasoning. Garnish with thyme sprigs and serve.

mediterranean lamb with apricots & pistachios

ingredients

SERVES 4

pinch of saffron threads

2 tbsp almost-boiling water

1 lb/450 g lean boneless
  lamb, such as leg steaks

1$^1/_2$ tbsp all-purpose flour

1 tsp ground coriander

$^1/_2$ tsp ground cumin

$^1/_2$ tsp ground allspice

1 tbsp olive oil

1 onion, chopped

2–3 garlic cloves, chopped

scant 2 cups lamb stock or
  chicken stock

1 cinnamon stick, bruised

$^1/_2$ cup dried apricots,
  coarsely chopped

$^3/_4$ zucchini, sliced into half
  circles

6–8 cherry tomatoes

1 tbsp chopped fresh cilantro

salt and pepper

2 tbsp coarsely chopped
  pistachios, to garnish

freshly cooked couscous,
  to serve

method

1 Put the saffron threads in a heatproof pitcher with the water and let stand for at least 10 minutes to steep. Trim off any fat or gristle from the lamb and cut into 1-inch/ 2.5-cm chunks. Mix the flour and spices together, then toss the lamb in the spiced flour until well coated and reserve any remaining spiced flour.

2 Heat the oil in a large heavy-bottom pan and cook the onion and garlic, stirring frequently, for 5 minutes, or until softened. Add the lamb and cook over high heat, stirring frequently, for 3 minutes, or until browned on all sides and sealed. Sprinkle in the reserved spiced flour and cook, stirring constantly, for 2 minutes, then remove from the heat.

3 Gradually stir in the stock and the saffron with its soaking liquid, then return to the heat and bring to a boil, stirring. Add the cinnamon stick and apricots. Reduce the heat, then cover and simmer, stirring occasionally, for 1 hour.

4 Add the zucchini and tomatoes and cook for an additional 15 minutes. Discard the cinnamon stick. Stir in the fresh cilantro and season to taste with salt and pepper. Sprinkle with the pistachios and serve with couscous.

cinnamon lamb casserole

ingredients

SERVES 6

2 tbsp all-purpose flour

2 lb 4 oz/1 kg lean boneless
lamb, cubed

2 tbsp olive oil

2 large onions, sliced

1 garlic clove, finely chopped

$1^{1}/_{4}$ cups full-bodied red wine

2 tbsp red wine vinegar

14 oz/400 g canned chopped
tomatoes

generous $^{1}/_{3}$ cup seedless
raisins

1 tbsp ground cinnamon

pinch of sugar

1 bay leaf

paprika, to garnish

topping

$^{2}/_{3}$ cup plain yogurt

2 garlic cloves, crushed

salt and pepper

method

1 Season the flour with salt and pepper to taste and put it with the lamb in a plastic bag, then hold the top closed and shake until the lamb cubes are lightly coated all over. Remove the lamb from the bag, then shake off any excess flour and set aside.

2 Heat the oil in a large flameproof casserole and cook the onions and garlic, stirring frequently, for 5 minutes, or until softened. Add the lamb and cook over high heat, stirring frequently, for 5 minutes, or until browned on all sides and sealed.

3 Stir the wine, vinegar, and tomatoes and their juice into the casserole, scraping any sediment from the bottom of the casserole, and bring to a boil. Reduce the heat and add the raisins, cinnamon, sugar, and bay leaf. Season to taste with salt and pepper. Cover and simmer gently for 2 hours, or until the lamb is tender.

4 Meanwhile, make the topping. Put the yogurt into a small serving bowl, then stir in the garlic and season to taste with salt and pepper. Cover and chill in the refrigerator until required.

5 Remove the bay leaf from the casserole and discard. Spoon into serving bowls, top with spoonfuls of the garlicky yogurt, and sprinkle over a little paprika. Serve hot.

country lamb casserole

ingredients

SERVES 6

2 tbsp corn oil

4 lb 8 oz/2 kg boneless leg of
   lamb, cut into 1-inch/
   2.5-cm cubes

6 leeks, sliced

1 tbsp all-purpose flour

$^2/_3$ cup rosé wine

1$^1/_4$ cups chicken stock

1 tbsp tomato paste

1 tbsp sugar

2 tbsp chopped fresh mint,
   plus extra sprigs to garnish

$^2/_3$ cup dried apricots, chopped

2 lb 4 oz/1 kg potatoes, sliced

3 tbsp melted unsalted butter

salt and pepper

method

1 Preheat the oven to 350°F/180°C. Heat the oil in a large flameproof casserole. Add the lamb in batches and cook over medium heat, stirring, for 5–8 minutes, or until browned. Transfer to a plate.

2 Add the leeks to the casserole and cook, stirring occasionally, for 5 minutes, or until softened. Sprinkle in the flour and cook, stirring, for 1 minute. Pour in the wine and stock and bring to a boil, stirring. Stir in the tomato paste, sugar, chopped mint, and apricots and season to taste with salt and pepper.

3 Return the lamb to the casserole and stir. Arrange the potato slices on top and brush with the melted butter. Cover and bake in the preheated oven for 1$^1/_2$ hours.

4 Increase the oven temperature to 400°F/200°C, uncover the casserole, and bake for an additional 30 minutes, or until the potato topping is golden brown. Serve immediately, garnished with mint sprigs.

lamb with pears

ingredients

SERVES 4

1 tbsp olive oil

2 lb 4 oz/1 kg best end-of-neck lamb cutlets, trimmed of visible fat

6 pears, peeled, cored, and cut into quarters

1 tsp ground ginger

4 potatoes, diced

4 tbsp hard cider

1 lb/450 g green beans

salt and pepper

2 tbsp snipped fresh chives, to garnish

method

1 Preheat the oven to 325°F/160°C. Heat the oil in a flameproof casserole over medium heat. Add the lamb and cook, turning frequently, for 5–10 minutes, or until browned on all sides.

2 Arrange the pear pieces on top, then sprinkle over the ginger. Cover with the potatoes. Pour in the cider and season to taste with salt and pepper. Cover and cook in the preheated oven for 1$1/4$ hours.

3 Trim the stem ends of the green beans. Remove the casserole from the oven and add the beans, then re-cover and return to the oven for an additional 30 minutes. Taste and adjust the seasoning and sprinkle with the chives. Serve immediately.

azerbaijani lamb pilaf

ingredients

SERVES 4

2–3 tbsp vegetable oil

1 lb 7 oz/650 g boneless
 lamb shoulder, cut into
 1-inch/2.5-cm cubes

2 onions, coarsely chopped

1 tsp ground cumin

7 oz/200 g risotto rice

1 tbsp tomato paste

1 tsp saffron threads

scant $1/2$ cup pomegranate
 juice

scant $3^{1}/2$ cups lamb stock,
 chicken stock, or water

$2/3$ cup dried apricots or
 prunes, halved

2 tbsp raisins

salt and pepper

shredded fresh mint and
 watercress, to serve

method

1 Heat the oil in a large flameproof casserole or pan over high heat. Add the lamb, in batches, and cook over high heat, turning frequently, for 7 minutes, or until lightly browned.

2 Add the onions, reduce the heat to medium, and cook for 2 minutes, or until beginning to soften. Add the cumin and rice and cook, stirring to coat, for 2 minutes, or until the rice is translucent. Stir in the tomato paste and the saffron threads.

3 Add the pomegranate juice and stock. Bring to a boil, stirring. Stir in the apricots and raisins. Reduce the heat to low, cover, and simmer for 20–25 minutes, or until the lamb and rice are tender and all of the liquid has been absorbed.

4 Season to taste with salt and pepper, then sprinkle the shredded mint and watercress over the pilaf and serve straight from the casserole.

pot-roast pork

ingredients

SERVES 4

1 tbsp corn oil

4 tbsp butter

2 lb 4 oz/1 kg boned and
    rolled pork loin

4 shallots, chopped

6 juniper berries

2 fresh thyme sprigs, plus
    extra to garnish

$^2/_3$ cup hard cider

$^2/_3$ cup chicken stock or water

8 celery stalks, chopped

2 tbsp all-purpose flour

$^2/_3$ cup heavy cream

salt and pepper

freshly cooked peas, to serve

method

1 Heat the oil with half the butter in a heavy-bottom pan or flameproof casserole. Add the pork and cook over medium heat, turning frequently, for 5–10 minutes, or until browned. Transfer to a plate.

2 Add the shallots to the pan and cook, stirring frequently, for 5 minutes, or until softened. Add the juniper berries and thyme sprigs and return the pork to the pan, with any juices that have collected on the plate. Pour in the cider and stock, season to taste with salt and pepper, then cover and simmer for 30 minutes. Turn the pork over and add the celery. Re-cover the pan and cook for an additional 40 minutes.

3 Meanwhile, make a beurre manié by mashing the remaining butter with the flour in a small bowl. Transfer the pork and celery to a platter with a slotted spoon and keep warm. Remove and discard the juniper berries and thyme. Whisk the beurre manié, a little at a time, into the simmering cooking liquid. Cook, stirring constantly, for 2 minutes, then stir in the cream and bring to a boil.

4 Slice the pork and spoon a little of the sauce over it. Garnish with thyme sprigs and serve immediately with the reserved celery, the peas, and the remaining sauce.

pork & vegetable stew

ingredients

SERVES 4

1 lb/450 g lean boneless pork

1^1/$_2$ tbsp all-purpose flour

1 tsp ground coriander

1 tsp ground cumin

1^1/$_2$ tsp ground cinnamon

1 tbsp olive oil

1 onion, chopped

14 oz/400 g canned chopped
   tomatoes

2 tbsp tomato paste

1^1/$_4$–scant 2 cups chicken
   stock

4 carrots, chopped

12 oz/350 g squash, such as
   kabocha, peeled, seeded,
   and chopped

1 large leek, sliced, blanched,
   and drained

4 oz/115 g okra, trimmed and
   sliced

salt and pepper

fresh parsley sprigs, to garnish

freshly cooked couscous,
   to serve

method

1 Trim off any fat or gristle from the pork and cut into thin strips about 2 inches/5 cm long. Mix the flour and spices together. Toss the pork in the spiced flour until well coated and reserve any remaining spiced flour.

2 Heat the oil in a large heavy-bottom pan and cook the onion, stirring frequently, for 5 minutes, or until softened. Add the pork and cook over high heat, stirring frequently, for 5 minutes, or until browned on all sides and sealed. Sprinkle in the reserved spiced flour and cook, stirring constantly, for 2 minutes, then remove from the heat.

3 Gradually add the tomatoes to the pan. Blend the tomato paste with a little of the stock in a pitcher and gradually stir into the pan, then stir in half the remaining stock.

4 Add the carrots, then return to the heat and bring to a boil, stirring. Reduce the heat, then cover and simmer, stirring occasionally, for 1^1/$_2$ hours. Add the squash and cook for an additional 15 minutes.

5 Add the leek and okra, and the remaining stock if you prefer a thinner sauce. Simmer for an additional 15 minutes, or until the pork and vegetables are tender. Season to taste with salt and pepper, then garnish with parsley sprigs and serve with couscous.

pork with red cabbage

ingredients

SERVES 4

1 tbsp corn oil

1 lb 10 oz/750 g boned and
    rolled pork loin

1 onion, finely chopped

1 lb 2 oz/500 g red cabbage,
    thick stems removed and
    leaves shredded

2 large baking apples, peeled,
    cored, and sliced

3 cloves

1 tsp brown sugar

3 tbsp lemon juice, and a thinly
    pared strip of lemon rind

lemon wedges, to garnish

method

1 Preheat the oven to 325°F/160°C. Heat the oil in a flameproof casserole. Add the pork and cook over medium heat, turning frequently, for 5–10 minutes, until browned. Transfer to a plate.

2 Add the onion to the casserole and cook over low heat, stirring occasionally, for 5 minutes, or until softened. Add the cabbage, in batches, and cook, stirring, for 2 minutes. Transfer each batch (mixed with some onion) into a bowl with a slotted spoon.

3 Add the apple slices, cloves, and sugar to the bowl and mix well, then place about half the mixture in the bottom of the casserole. Top with the pork and add the remaining cabbage mixture. Sprinkle in the lemon juice and add the strip of rind. Cover and cook in the preheated oven for 1^1/2 hours.

4 Transfer the pork to a plate. Transfer the cabbage mixture to the plate with a slotted spoon and keep warm. Bring the cooking juices to a boil over high heat and reduce slightly. Slice the pork and arrange on warmed serving plates, surrounded with the cabbage mixture. Spoon the cooking juices over the meat and serve with lemon wedges.

paprika pork

ingredients

SERVES 4

1 lb 8 oz/675 g pork
   tenderloin
2 tbsp corn oil
2 tbsp butter
1 onion, chopped
1 tbsp paprika
2$\frac{1}{2}$ tbsp all-purpose flour
1$\frac{1}{4}$ cups chicken stock
4 tbsp dry sherry
4 oz/115 g button
   mushrooms, sliced
$\frac{2}{3}$ cup sour cream
salt and pepper

method

1 Cut the pork into 1$\frac{1}{2}$-inch/4-cm cubes.
Heat the oil and butter in a large pan. Add the
pork and cook over medium heat, stirring, for
5 minutes, or until browned. Transfer to a
plate with a slotted spoon.

2 Add the onion to the pan and cook, stirring
occasionally, for 5 minutes, or until softened.
Stir in the paprika and flour and cook, stirring
constantly, for 2 minutes. Gradually stir in the
stock and bring to a boil, stirring constantly.

3 Return the pork to the pan, add the sherry
and mushrooms, and season to taste with
salt and pepper. Cover and simmer gently
for 20 minutes, or until the pork is tender.
Stir in the sour cream and serve.

pork chops with bell peppers & corn

ingredients

SERVES 4

1 tbsp corn oil

4 pork chops, trimmed of
   visible fat

1 onion, chopped

1 garlic clove, finely chopped

1 green bell pepper, seeded
   and sliced

1 red bell pepper, seeded and
   sliced

11$^{1}/_{2}$ oz/325 g canned corn
   kernels

1 tbsp chopped fresh parsley

salt and pepper

mashed potatoes, to serve

method

1 Heat the oil in a large flameproof casserole. Add the pork chops in batches and cook over medium heat, turning occasionally, for 5 minutes, or until browned. Transfer the chops to a plate with a slotted spoon.

2 Add the onion to the casserole and cook, stirring occasionally, for 5 minutes, or until softened. Add the garlic and bell peppers and cook, stirring occasionally, for an additional 5 minutes. Stir in the corn kernels and their juices and the parsley and season to taste with salt and pepper.

3 Return the chops to the casserole, spooning the vegetable mixture over them. Cover and simmer for 30 minutes, or until tender. Serve immediately with mashed potatoes.

sausage & bean casserole

ingredients

SERVES 4

8 Italian sausages

3 tbsp olive oil

1 large onion, chopped

2 garlic cloves, chopped

1 green bell pepper, seeded
and sliced

2 small fresh tomatoes,
skinned and chopped,
or 14 oz/400 g canned
chopped tomatoes

2 tbsp sun-dried tomato paste

14 oz/400 g canned
cannellini beans, drained

mashed potatoes, to serve

method

1 Prick the sausages all over with a fork. Heat 2 tablespoons of the oil in a large heavy-bottom skillet. Add the sausages and cook over low heat, turning frequently, for 10–15 minutes, until evenly browned and cooked through. Remove them from the skillet and keep warm. Drain off the oil and wipe out the skillet with paper towels.

2 Heat the remaining oil in the skillet. Add the onion, garlic, and bell pepper to the skillet and cook for 5 minutes, stirring occasionally, or until softened.

3 Add the tomatoes to the skillet and let the mixture simmer for about 5 minutes, stirring occasionally, or until slightly reduced and thickened.

4 Stir the sun-dried tomato paste, cannellini beans, and sausages into the mixture in the skillet. Cook for 4–5 minutes, or until the mixture is piping hot. Add 4–5 tablespoons of water if the mixture becomes too dry during cooking.

5 Transfer to serving plates and serve with mashed potatoes.

asian pork

ingredients

SERVES 4

1 lb/450 g lean boneless pork

1$\frac{1}{2}$ tbsp all-purpose flour

1–2 tbsp olive oil

1 onion, cut into small wedges

2–3 garlic cloves, chopped

1-inch/2.5-cm piece fresh
ginger, peeled and grated

1 tbsp tomato paste

1$\frac{1}{4}$ cups chicken stock

8 oz/225 g canned pineapple
chunks in natural juice

1–1$\frac{1}{2}$ tbsp dark soy sauce

1 red bell pepper, seeded
and sliced

1 green bell pepper, seeded
and sliced

1$\frac{1}{2}$ tbsp balsamic vinegar

4 scallions, diagonally sliced,
to garnish

method

1 Trim off any fat or gristle from the pork and cut into 1-inch/2.5-cm chunks. Toss the pork in the flour until well coated and reserve any remaining flour.

2 Heat the oil in a large heavy-bottom pan and cook the onion, garlic, and ginger, stirring frequently, for 5 minutes, or until softened. Add the pork and cook over high heat, stirring frequently, for 5 minutes, or until browned on all sides and sealed. Sprinkle in the reserved flour and cook, stirring constantly, for 2 minutes, then remove from the heat.

3 Blend the tomato paste with the stock in a heatproof pitcher and gradually stir into the pan. Drain the pineapple, reserving both the fruit and juice, and stir the juice into the pan.

4 Add the soy sauce to the pan, then return to the heat and bring to a boil, stirring. Reduce the heat, then cover and simmer, stirring occasionally, for 1 hour. Add the bell peppers and cook for an additional 15 minutes, or until the pork is tender. Stir in the vinegar and the reserved pineapple and heat through for 5 minutes. Serve sprinkled with the scallions.

red curry pork with bell pepper

ingredients

SERVES 4

2 tbsp vegetable oil or
　　peanut oil
1 onion, coarsely chopped
2 garlic cloves, chopped
1 lb/450 g pork tenderloin,
　　thickly sliced
1 red bell pepper, seeded and
　　cut into squares
6 oz/175 g button
　　mushrooms, quartered
2 tbsp Thai red curry paste
2$\frac{1}{2}$ cups coconut cream
1 tsp vegetable bouillon
　　powder
2 tbsp Thai soy sauce
4 tomatoes, peeled, seeded,
　　and chopped
handful of fresh cilantro,
　　chopped
freshly cooked noodles,
　　to serve

method

1 Heat the oil in a wok or large skillet and sauté the onion and garlic for 1–2 minutes, until they are softened but not browned.

2 Add the pork and stir-fry for 2–3 minutes, until browned all over. Add the bell pepper, mushrooms, and curry paste.

3 Add the coconut cream to the wok with bouillon powder and soy sauce. Bring to a boil and let simmer for 4–5 minutes, until the liquid has reduced and thickened.

4 Add the tomatoes and cilantro and cook for 1–2 minutes before serving with noodles.

poultry

Poultry, particularly chicken, is extremely versatile and goes well with a wide range of other ingredients and flavors. It's also suited to all kinds of one-pot cooking—from stews and casseroles to roasts and risottos. It can be cooked whole, cut into quarters or smaller pieces on the bone, or boned and diced. Because almost everyone likes it, chicken is a great choice for family meals.

Combining chicken with different herbs, spices, and other flavorings gives each dish individuality, so there's no risk of getting bored. A Middle Eastern stew of diced chicken meat, vegetables, chickpeas, and apricots, lightly spiced with cumin and cinnamon, couldn't be more different from a whole bird roasted with potatoes, bell peppers, and zucchini, for example. It is just as good cooked in red or white wine as it is with chiles, ginger, and coconut milk.

Turkey and duck recipes add variety and a hint of something special to the menu, making these dishes ideal for informal entertaining. Because both turkey and duck have a tendency to dry out during cooking, one-pot recipes incorporating a richly flavored sauce will guarantee success. Fillets, steaks, and duck legs are inexpensive so you'll find they will easily fit your family budget while adding variety to your daily menus.

chicken & barley stew

ingredients

SERVES 4

2 tbsp vegetable oil

8 small skinless chicken thighs

generous 2 cups chicken stock

scant $1/2$ cup pearl barley, rinsed and drained

7 small new potatoes, scrubbed and cut in half lengthwise

2 large carrots, peeled and sliced

1 leek, trimmed and sliced

2 shallots, sliced

1 tbsp tomato paste

1 bay leaf

1 zucchini, trimmed and sliced

2 tbsp chopped fresh flat-leaf parsley, plus extra sprigs to garnish

2 tbsp all-purpose flour

salt and pepper

crusty bread, to serve

method

1 Heat the oil in a large saucepan over medium heat. Add the chicken and cook for 3 minutes, then turn over and cook on the other side for an additional 2 minutes. Add the stock, pearl barley, potatoes, carrots, leek, shallots, tomato paste, and bay leaf. Bring to a boil, lower the heat, and simmer for 30 minutes.

2 Add the zucchini and chopped parsley, cover the pan, and cook for an additional 20 minutes, or until the chicken is cooked through. Remove the bay leaf and discard.

3 In a separate bowl, mix the flour with 4 tablespoons of water to make a smooth paste. Add it to the stew and cook, stirring, over low heat for an additional 5 minutes. Season to taste with salt and pepper.

4 Remove from the heat, ladle into individual serving bowls, and garnish with parsley sprigs. Serve with crusty bread.

coq au vin

ingredients

SERVES 4

4 tbsp butter

2 tbsp olive oil

4 lb/1.8 kg chicken pieces

4 oz/115 g rindless smoked
bacon, cut into strips

4 oz/115 g pearl onions,
peeled

4 oz/115 g cremini
mushrooms, halved

2 garlic cloves, finely
chopped

2 tbsp brandy

scant 1 cup red wine

1^1/$_4$ cups chicken stock

1 bouquet garni

2 tbsp all-purpose flour

salt and pepper

bay leaves, to garnish

method

1 Melt half the butter with the olive oil in a large flameproof casserole. Add the chicken and cook over medium heat, stirring, for 8–10 minutes, or until golden brown. Add the bacon, onions, mushrooms, and garlic.

2 Pour in the brandy and set it alight with a match or taper. When the flames have died down, add the wine, stock, and bouquet garni and season to taste with salt and pepper. Bring to a boil, reduce the heat, and simmer gently for 1 hour, or until the chicken pieces are cooked through and tender.

3 Meanwhile, make a beurre manié by mashing the remaining butter with the flour in a small bowl.

4 Remove the bouquet garni from the casserole and discard. Transfer the chicken to a large plate and keep warm. Stir the beurre manié into the casserole, a little at a time. Bring to a boil, then return the chicken to the casserole to warm through. Serve immediately, garnished with bay leaves.

all-in-one roast chicken

ingredients

SERVES 6

1 chicken, weighing
　　5 lb 8 oz/2.5 kg

a few fresh rosemary sprigs

$^3/_4$ cup coarsely grated feta
　　cheese

2 tbsp sun-dried tomato paste

4 tbsp butter, softened

1 bulb garlic

2 lb 4 oz/1 kg new potatoes,
　　halved if large

1 each red, green, and yellow
　　bell pepper, seeded and
　　cut into chunks

3 zucchini, thinly sliced

2 tbsp olive oil

2 tbsp all-purpose flour

$2^1/_2$ cups chicken stock

salt and pepper

method

1 Preheat the oven to 375°F/190°C. Rinse the chicken and drain well. Carefully cut between the skin and the top of the breasts. Slide a finger into the slit and carefully enlarge it to form a pocket. Continue until the skin is lifted away from both breasts and the top of the legs.

2 Chop the leaves from 3 rosemary stems. Mix with the feta cheese, sun-dried tomato paste, butter, and pepper to taste, then spoon under the skin. Put the chicken in a large roasting pan, cover with foil, and cook in the preheated oven for 40 minutes.

3 Break the garlic bulb into cloves, but do not peel. Remove the roasting pan from the oven and add the vegetables and garlic. Drizzle with the oil, tuck in a few rosemary sprigs, and season to taste with salt and pepper. Cook for an additional 40 minutes, then remove the foil. Return to the oven and cook for an additional 40 minutes, until the juices run clear when a skewer is inserted into the thickest part of the meat.

4 Transfer the chicken and vegetables to a serving platter. Spoon the fat out of the roasting pan and stir the flour into the remaining cooking juices. Place the roasting pan on top of the stove and cook over medium heat for 2 minutes, then gradually stir in the stock. Bring to a boil, stirring until thickened. Serve.

spicy aromatic chicken

ingredients

SERVES 4

4–8 chicken pieces, skinned

1/2 lemon, cut into wedges

4 tbsp olive oil

1 onion, coarsely chopped

2 large garlic cloves, finely
   chopped

1/2 cup dry white wine

14 oz/400 g canned chopped
   tomatoes

pinch of sugar

1/2 tsp ground cinnamon

1/2 tsp ground cloves

1/2 tsp ground allspice

14 oz/400 g canned artichoke
   hearts or okra, drained

8 black olives, pitted

salt and pepper

method

1 Rub the chicken pieces with the lemon. Heat the oil in a large flameproof casserole or lidded skillet. Add the onion and garlic and fry for 5 minutes, until softened. Add the chicken pieces and fry for 5–10 minutes, until browned on all sides.

2 Pour in the wine and add the tomatoes with their juice, the sugar, cinnamon, cloves, allspice, and salt and pepper to taste and bring to a boil. Cover the casserole and simmer for 45 minutes–1 hour, until the chicken is tender.

3 Meanwhile, if using artichoke hearts, cut them in half. Add the artichokes or okra and the olives to the casserole 10 minutes before the end of cooking, and continue to simmer until heated through. Serve hot.

chicken, corn & lima bean stew

ingredients

SERVES 6

4 lb/1.8 kg chicken pieces

2 tbsp paprika

2 tbsp olive oil

2 tbsp butter

1 lb/450 g onions, chopped

2 yellow bell peppers, seeded
  and chopped

14 oz/400 g canned chopped
  tomatoes

scant 1 cup dry white wine

generous 1¾ cups chicken
  stock

1 tbsp Worcestershire sauce

½ tsp Tabasco sauce

1 tbsp finely chopped fresh
  parsley, plus extra sprigs
  to garnish

11½ oz/325 g canned corn
  kernels, drained

15 oz/425 g canned lima
  beans, drained and rinsed

2 tbsp all-purpose flour

4 tbsp water

salt

method

1 Season the chicken pieces with salt to taste and dust with paprika.

2 Heat the oil and butter in a flameproof casserole or large pan. Add the chicken pieces and cook over medium heat, turning, for 10–15 minutes, or until golden. Transfer to a plate with a slotted spoon.

3 Add the onions and bell peppers to the casserole. Cook over low heat, stirring occasionally, for 5 minutes, or until softened. Add the tomatoes, wine, stock, Worcestershire sauce, Tabasco sauce, and chopped parsley and bring to a boil, stirring. Return the chicken to the casserole, cover, and simmer, stirring occasionally, for 30 minutes.

4 Add the corn and beans to the casserole, partially re-cover, and simmer for an additional 30 minutes. Place the flour and water in a small bowl and mix to make a paste. Stir a ladleful of the cooking liquid into the paste, then stir it into the stew. Cook, stirring frequently, for 5 minutes. Serve, garnished with parsley sprigs.

chicken in white wine

ingredients

SERVES 4

4 tbsp butter

2 tbsp olive oil

2 thick, rindless, lean bacon strips, chopped

4 oz/115 g pearl onions, peeled

1 garlic clove, finely chopped

4 lb/1.8 kg chicken pieces

$1^3/_4$ cups dry white wine

$1^1/_4$ cups chicken stock

1 bouquet garni

4 oz/115 g button mushrooms

$2^1/_2$ tbsp all-purpose flour

salt and pepper

fresh herb sprigs, to garnish

method

1 Preheat the oven to 325°F/160°C. Melt half the butter with the oil in a flameproof casserole. Add the bacon and cook over medium heat, stirring, for 5–10 minutes, or until golden brown. Transfer the bacon to a large plate. Add the onions and garlic to the casserole and cook over low heat, stirring occasionally, for 10 minutes, or until golden. Transfer to the plate. Add the chicken and cook over medium heat, stirring constantly, for 8–10 minutes, or until golden. Transfer to the plate.

2 Drain off any excess fat from the casserole. Stir in the wine and stock and bring to a boil, scraping any sediment off the bottom. Add the bouquet garni and season to taste with salt and pepper. Return the bacon, onions, garlic, and chicken to the casserole. Cover and cook in the preheated oven for 1 hour.

3 Add the mushrooms, re-cover, and cook for 15 minutes. Meanwhile, make a beurre manié by mashing the remaining butter with the flour in a small bowl.

4 Remove the casserole from the oven and set over medium heat. Discard the bouquet garni. Whisk in the beurre manié, a little at a time. Bring to a boil, stirring constantly, then serve, garnished with fresh herb sprigs.

hunter's chicken

ingredients

SERVES 4

1 tbsp unsalted butter

2 tbsp olive oil

4 lb/1.8 kg skinned, unboned
   chicken portions

2 red onions, sliced

2 garlic cloves, finely
   chopped

14 oz/400 g canned chopped
   tomatoes

2 tbsp chopped fresh flat-leaf
   parsley

6 fresh basil leaves, torn

1 tbsp sun-dried tomato paste

$2/3$ cup red wine

8 oz/225 g button
   mushrooms, sliced

salt and pepper

method

1 Preheat the oven to 325°F/160°C. Heat the butter and oil in a flameproof casserole and cook the chicken over medium–high heat, turning frequently, for 10 minutes, or until golden all over and sealed. Using a slotted spoon, transfer to a plate.

2 Add the onions and garlic to the casserole and cook over low heat, stirring occasionally, for 10 minutes, or until softened and golden. Add the tomatoes with their juice, the herbs, sun-dried tomato paste, and wine, and season to taste with salt and pepper. Bring to a boil, then return the chicken portions to the casserole, pushing them down into the sauce.

3 Cover and cook in the preheated oven for 50 minutes. Add the mushrooms and cook for an additional 10 minutes, or until the chicken is tender and the juices run clear when a skewer is inserted into the thickest part of the meat. Serve immediately.

chicken basquaise

ingredients

SERVES 4–5

1 chicken, weighing 3 lb/
   1.3 kg, cut into 8 pieces
2 tbsp all-purpose flour
3 tbsp olive oil
1 Bermuda onion, thickly
   sliced
2 red or yellow bell peppers,
   seeded and cut lengthwise
   into thick strips
2 garlic cloves
$5^{1}/_{2}$ oz/150 g spicy chorizo
   sausage, peeled and cut
   into $^{1}/_{2}$-inch/1-cm pieces
1 tbsp tomato paste
1 cup long-grain white rice
2 cups chicken stock
1 tsp chile flakes
$^{1}/_{2}$ tsp dried thyme
$^{3}/_{4}$ cup diced prosciutto
12 dry-cured black olives
2 tbsp chopped fresh flat-leaf
   parsley
salt and pepper

method

1 Pat the chicken pieces dry with paper towels. Put the flour in a plastic bag, season to taste with salt and pepper, and add the chicken pieces. Seal the bag and shake to coat the chicken.

2 Heat 2 tablespoons of the oil in a large flameproof casserole over medium–high heat. Add the chicken and cook, turning frequently, for about 15 minutes, until well browned all over. Transfer to a plate.

3 Heat the remaining oil in the casserole and add the onion and bell peppers. Reduce the heat to medium and stir-fry until beginning to color and soften. Add the garlic, chorizo, and tomato paste and cook, stirring constantly, for about 3 minutes. Add the rice and cook, stirring to coat, for about 2 minutes, until the rice is translucent.

4 Add the stock, chile flakes, and thyme, season to taste with salt and pepper, and stir well. Bring to a boil. Return the chicken to the casserole, pressing it gently into the rice. Cover and cook over very low heat for about 45 minutes, until the chicken is cooked through and the rice is tender.

5 Gently stir the prosciutto, olives, and half the parsley into the rice mixture. Re-cover and heat through for an additional 5 minutes. Sprinkle with the remaining parsley and serve immediately.

sunshine chicken

ingredients

SERVES 4

1 lb/450 g skinless, boneless chicken

1$\frac{1}{2}$ tbsp all-purpose flour

1 tbsp olive oil

1 onion, cut into wedges

2 celery stalks, sliced

$\frac{2}{3}$ cup orange juice

1$\frac{1}{4}$ cups chicken stock

1 tbsp light soy sauce

1–2 tsp honey

1 tbsp grated orange rind

1 orange bell pepper, seeded and chopped

1 zucchini, sliced into half circles

2 small corn cobs, halved, or 3$\frac{1}{2}$ oz/100 g baby corn

1 orange, peeled and segmented

salt and pepper

1 tbsp chopped fresh parsley, to garnish

method

1 Lightly rinse the chicken and pat dry with paper towels. Cut into bite-size pieces. Season the flour well with salt and pepper. Toss the chicken in the seasoned flour until well coated and reserve any remaining seasoned flour.

2 Heat the oil in a large heavy-bottom skillet and cook the chicken over high heat, stirring frequently, for 5 minutes, or until golden on all sides and sealed. Using a slotted spoon, transfer to a plate.

3 Add the onion and celery to the skillet and cook over medium heat, stirring frequently, for 5 minutes, or until softened. Sprinkle in the reserved seasoned flour and cook, stirring constantly, for 2 minutes, then remove from the heat. Gradually stir in the orange juice, stock, soy sauce, and honey followed by the orange rind, then return to the heat and bring to a boil, stirring.

4 Return the chicken to the skillet. Reduce the heat, then cover and simmer, stirring occasionally, for 15 minutes. Add the orange bell pepper, zucchini, and corn cobs and simmer for an additional 10 minutes, or until the chicken and vegetables are tender. Add the orange segments, then stir well and heat through for 1 minute. Serve garnished with the parsley.

thai green chicken curry

ingredients

SERVES 4

2 tbsp peanut oil or corn oil

1 lb 2 oz/500 g skinless, boneless chicken breasts, cut into cubes

2 kaffir lime leaves, coarsely torn

1 lemongrass stalk, finely chopped

1 cup canned coconut milk

16 baby eggplants, halved

2 tbsp Thai fish sauce

fresh Thai basil sprigs and thinly sliced kaffir lime leaves, to garnish

green curry paste

16 fresh green chiles

2 shallots, sliced

4 kaffir lime leaves

1 lemongrass stalk, chopped

2 garlic cloves, chopped

1 tsp cumin seeds

1 tsp coriander seeds

1 tbsp grated fresh ginger or galangal

1 tsp grated lime rind

5 black peppercorns

1 tbsp sugar

2 tbsp peanut oil or corn oil

method

1 First make the curry paste. Seed the chiles, if you like, and coarsely chop. Place all the paste ingredients, except the oil, in a mortar and pound with a pestle. Alternatively, process in a food processor. Gradually blend in the oil. Set aside.

2 Heat a wok or large heavy-bottom skillet and add the oil. When the oil is hot, add 2 tablespoons of the curry paste and stir-fry briefly until all the aromas are released.

3 Add the chicken, lime leaves, and lemongrass and stir-fry for 3–4 minutes, until the meat begins to color. Add the coconut milk and eggplants and let simmer gently for 8–10 minutes, or until tender.

4 Stir in the fish sauce and serve immediately, garnished with Thai basil sprigs and shredded lime leaves.

chicken tagine

ingredients

SERVES 4

1 tbsp olive oil

1 onion, cut into small wedges

2–4 garlic cloves, sliced

1 lb/450 g skinless, boneless chicken breast, diced

1 tsp ground cumin

2 cinnamon sticks, lightly bruised

1 tbsp whole-wheat flour

1 small eggplant, diced

1 red bell pepper, seeded and chopped

$1^1/_2$ cups sliced button mushrooms

1 tbsp tomato paste

$2^1/_2$ cups chicken stock

10 oz/280 g canned chickpeas, drained and rinsed

$^1/_3$ cup plumped dried apricots, chopped

salt and pepper

1 tbsp chopped fresh cilantro, to garnish

method

1 Heat the oil in a large pan over medium heat, add the onion and garlic, and cook for 3 minutes, stirring frequently. Add the chicken and cook, stirring constantly, for an additional 5 minutes, or until sealed on all sides. Add the cumin and cinnamon sticks to the pan halfway through sealing the chicken.

2 Sprinkle in the flour and cook, stirring constantly, for 2 minutes.

3 Add the eggplant, red bell pepper, and mushrooms and cook for an additional 2 minutes, stirring constantly.

4 Blend the tomato paste with the stock, stir into the pan, and bring to a boil. Reduce the heat and add the chickpeas and apricots. Cover and let simmer for 15–20 minutes, or until the chicken is tender.

5 Season to taste with salt and pepper and serve immediately, sprinkled with cilantro.

mexican chicken, chile & potato pot

ingredients

SERVES 4

2 tbsp vegetable oil

1 lb/450 g boneless, skinless chicken breasts, cubed

1 onion, finely chopped

1 green bell pepper, seeded and finely chopped

1 potato, diced

1 sweet potato, diced

2 garlic cloves, very finely chopped

1–2 fresh green chiles, seeded and very finely chopped

7 oz/200 g canned chopped tomatoes

$1/2$ tsp dried oregano

$1/2$ tsp salt

$1/2$ tsp pepper

4 tbsp chopped fresh cilantro

2 cups chicken stock

method

1 Heat the oil in a large heavy-bottom pan over medium–high heat. Cook the chicken until lightly browned.

2 Reduce the heat to medium. Add the onion, bell pepper, potato, and sweet potato. Cover and cook for 5 minutes, stirring occasionally, until the vegetables begin to soften.

3 Add the garlic and chiles. Cook for 1 minute. Stir in the tomatoes, oregano, salt, pepper, and 2 tablespoons of the cilantro. Cook for 1 minute.

4 Pour in the stock. Bring to a boil, then cover and simmer over low–medium heat for 15–20 minutes, or until the chicken is cooked through and the vegetables are tender.

5 Sprinkle with the remaining cilantro just before serving.

chicken jalfrezi

ingredients

SERVES 4

$^{1}/_{2}$ tsp cumin seeds

$^{1}/_{2}$ tsp coriander seeds

1 tsp mustard oil

3 tbsp vegetable oil

1 large onion, finely chopped

3 garlic cloves, crushed

1 tbsp tomato paste

2 tomatoes, peeled and
    chopped

1 tsp ground turmeric

$^{1}/_{2}$ tsp chili powder

$^{1}/_{2}$ tsp garam masala

1 tsp red wine vinegar

1 small red bell pepper,
    seeded and chopped

$^{3}/_{4}$ cup frozen fava beans

1 lb 2 oz/500 g cooked
    chicken, chopped

salt

fresh cilantro sprigs,
    to garnish

freshly cooked rice, to serve

method

1 Grind the cumin and coriander seeds in a mortar with a pestle, then reserve. Heat the mustard oil in a large heavy-bottom skillet over high heat for 1 minute, or until it begins to smoke. Add the vegetable oil, reduce the heat, and add the onion and garlic. Cook for 10 minutes, or until golden.

2 Add the tomato paste, tomatoes, turmeric, ground cumin and coriander seeds, chili powder, garam masala, and vinegar to the skillet. Stir the mixture until fragrant.

3 Add the bell pepper and fava beans and stir for an additional 2 minutes, or until the bell pepper is softened. Stir in the chicken and season to taste with salt, then simmer gently for 6–8 minutes, until the chicken is heated through and the beans are tender.

4 Transfer to warmed serving bowls, garnish with cilantro sprigs, and serve with freshly cooked rice.

balti chicken

ingredients

SERVES 6

3 tbsp ghee or vegetable oil

2 large onions, sliced

3 tomatoes, sliced

$1/2$ tsp nigella seeds

4 black peppercorns

2 cardamom pods

1 cinnamon stick

1 tsp chili powder

1 tsp garam masala

1 tsp garlic paste

1 tsp ginger paste

1 lb 9 oz/700 g skinless,
    boneless chicken breasts
    or thighs, diced

2 tbsp plain yogurt

2 tbsp chopped fresh cilantro,
    plus extra sprigs to garnish

2 fresh green chiles, seeded
    and finely chopped

2 tbsp lime juice

salt

method

1 Heat the ghee in a large heavy-bottom skillet. Add the onions and cook over low heat, stirring occasionally, for 10 minutes, or until golden. Add the tomatoes, nigella seeds, peppercorns, cardamom pods, cinnamon stick, chili powder, garam masala, garlic paste, and ginger paste and season to taste with salt. Cook, stirring constantly, for 5 minutes.

2 Add the chicken and cook, stirring constantly, for 5 minutes, or until well coated in the spice paste. Stir in the yogurt. Cover and let simmer, stirring occasionally, for 10 minutes.

3 Stir in the chopped cilantro, chiles, and lime juice. Transfer to a warmed serving dish, garnish with cilantro sprigs, and serve immediately.

chicken with garlic

ingredients

SERVES 4

4 tbsp all-purpose flour

Spanish paprika, either hot or
  smoked sweet, to taste

1 large chicken, about
  3 lb 12 oz/1.75 kg,
  cut into 8 pieces, rinsed,
  and patted dry

4–6 tbsp olive oil

24 large garlic cloves, peeled
  and halved

scant 2 cups chicken stock

4 tbsp dry white wine, such
  as white Rioja

2 fresh flat-leaf parsley sprigs,
  1 bay leaf, and 1 fresh
  thyme sprig

salt and pepper

fresh parsley and thyme
  leaves, to garnish

method

1 Sift the flour onto a large plate and season to taste with paprika and salt and pepper. Dredge the chicken pieces with the flour on both sides, shaking off the excess.

2 Heat 4 tablespoons of the oil in a large deep skillet or flameproof casserole over medium heat. Add the garlic and cook, stirring frequently, for about 2 minutes to flavor the oil. Remove with a slotted spoon and set aside to drain on paper towels.

3 Add as many chicken pieces, skin-side down, as will fit in a single layer. (Work in batches to avoid overcrowding the skillet, adding a little extra oil if necessary.) Cook for 5 minutes, until the skin is golden brown. Turn over and cook for an additional 5 minutes.

4 Pour off any excess oil. Return the garlic and chicken pieces to the skillet and add the stock, wine, and herbs. Bring to a boil, then reduce the heat, cover, and let simmer for 20–25 minutes, until the chicken is cooked through and tender and the garlic is very soft.

5 Transfer the chicken pieces to a serving platter and keep warm. Bring the cooking liquid to a boil and boil until reduced to about $1^1/2$ cups. Remove and discard the herbs. Taste and adjust the seasoning, if necessary.

6 Spoon the sauce and the garlic cloves over the chicken pieces. Garnish with the parsley and thyme leaves and serve.

louisiana chicken

ingredients

SERVES 4

5 tbsp corn oil

4 chicken portions

6 tbsp all-purpose flour

1 onion, chopped

2 celery stalks, sliced

1 green bell pepper, seeded
and chopped

2 garlic cloves, finely
chopped

2 tsp chopped fresh thyme,
plus extra to garnish

2 fresh red chiles, seeded
and finely chopped

14 oz/400 g canned chopped
tomatoes

1¹/₄ cups chicken stock

salt and pepper

method

1 Heat the oil in a large heavy-bottom pan or flameproof casserole. Add the chicken and cook over medium heat, stirring, for 5–10 minutes, or until golden. Transfer the chicken to a plate with a slotted spoon.

2 Stir the flour into the oil and cook over very low heat, stirring constantly, for 15 minutes, or until golden. Do not let it burn. Immediately add the onion, celery, and green bell pepper and cook, stirring constantly, for 2 minutes. Add the garlic, thyme, and chiles and cook, stirring, for 1 minute.

3 Stir in the tomatoes and their juices, then gradually stir in the stock. Return the chicken pieces to the pan, cover, and simmer for 45 minutes, or until the chicken is cooked through and tender. Season to taste with salt and pepper and transfer to warmed serving plates. Serve immediately, garnished with a sprinkling of chopped thyme.

chicken pepperonata

ingredients

SERVES 4

8 skinless chicken thighs

2 tbsp whole-wheat flour

2 tbsp olive oil

1 small onion, thinly sliced

1 garlic clove, crushed

1 each large red, yellow, and
    green bell peppers,
    seeded and thinly sliced

14 oz/400 g canned chopped
    tomatoes

1 tbsp chopped fresh oregano,
    plus extra to garnish

salt and pepper

crusty whole-wheat bread,
    to serve

method

1 Toss the chicken thighs in the flour, shaking off the excess.

2 Heat the oil in a wide skillet and fry the chicken quickly until sealed and lightly browned, then remove from the pan.

3 Add the onion to the pan and gently fry until softened. Add the garlic, bell peppers, tomatoes, and oregano, then bring to a boil, stirring.

4 Arrange the chicken over the vegetables, season well with salt and pepper, then cover the pan tightly and simmer for 20–25 minutes, or until the chicken is completely cooked and tender.

5 Taste and adjust the seasoning, adding salt and pepper if necessary, garnish with oregano, and serve with crusty whole-wheat bread.

chicken risotto with saffron

ingredients

SERVES 4

generous $1/2$ cup butter

2 lb/900 g skinless, boneless
chicken breasts, thinly
sliced

1 large onion, chopped

1 lb 2 oz/500 g risotto rice

$2/3$ cup white wine

1 tsp crumbled saffron
threads

generous $5^{1}/2$ cups boiling
chicken stock

$1/2$ cup freshly grated
Parmesan cheese

salt and pepper

method

1 Melt 4 tablespoons of the butter in a deep pan, add the chicken and onion, and cook, stirring frequently, for 8 minutes, or until golden brown.

2 Add the rice and mix to coat in the butter. Cook, stirring constantly for 2–3 minutes, or until the grains are translucent. Add the wine and cook, stirring constantly, for 1 minute until reduced.

3 Mix the saffron with 4 tablespoons of the hot stock. Add the liquid to the rice and cook, stirring constantly, until it is absorbed.

4 Gradually add the remaining hot stock, a ladleful at a time. Stir constantly and add more liquid as the rice absorbs each addition. Cook for 20 minutes, or until all the liquid is absorbed and the rice is creamy. Season to taste with salt and pepper.

5 Remove the risotto from the heat and add the remaining butter. Mix well, then stir in the Parmesan until it melts. Spoon the risotto onto warmed plates and serve immediately.

spicy turkey casserole

ingredients

SERVES 4

6 tbsp all-purpose flour

4 turkey breast fillets

3 tbsp corn oil

1 onion, thinly sliced

1 red bell pepper, seeded
and sliced

1¼ cups chicken stock

2 tbsp raisins

4 tomatoes, peeled, seeded,
and chopped

1 tsp chili powder

½ tsp ground cinnamon

pinch of ground cumin

1 oz/25 g semisweet
chocolate, finely chopped
or grated

salt and pepper

fresh cilantro sprigs,
to garnish

method

1 Preheat the oven to 325°F/160°C. Spread the flour on a plate and season to taste with salt and pepper. Coat the turkey fillets in the seasoned flour, shaking off any excess.

2 Heat the oil in a flameproof casserole. Add the turkey fillets and cook over medium heat, turning occasionally, for 5–10 minutes, or until golden. Transfer to a plate with a slotted spoon.

3 Add the onion and bell pepper to the casserole. Cook over low heat, stirring occasionally, for 5 minutes, or until softened. Sprinkle in any remaining seasoned flour and cook, stirring constantly, for 1 minute.

4 Gradually stir in the stock, then add the raisins, tomatoes, chili powder, cinnamon, cumin, and chocolate. Season to taste with salt and pepper. Bring to a boil, stirring constantly.

5 Return the turkey to the casserole, cover, and cook in the preheated oven for 50 minutes. Serve immediately, garnished with cilantro sprigs.

italian turkey steaks

ingredients

SERVES 4

1 tbsp olive oil

4 turkey scallops or steaks

2 red bell peppers

1 red onion

2 garlic cloves, finely
    chopped

1^1/$_4$ cups strained tomatoes

^{2}/$_3$ cup medium white wine

1 tbsp chopped fresh
    marjoram

14 oz/400 g canned
    cannellini beans, drained
    and rinsed

3 tbsp fresh white
    breadcrumbs

salt and pepper

fresh basil sprigs, to garnish

method

1 Heat the oil in a flameproof casserole or heavy-bottom skillet. Add the turkey scallops and cook over medium heat for 5–10 minutes, turning occasionally, until golden. Transfer to a plate.

2 Seed and slice the bell peppers. Slice the onion, add to the casserole with the bell peppers, and cook over low heat, stirring occasionally, for 5 minutes, or until softened. Add the garlic and cook for an additional 2 minutes.

3 Return the turkey to the casserole and add the strained tomatoes, wine, and marjoram. Season to taste with salt and pepper. Bring to a boil, then reduce the heat, cover, and simmer, stirring occasionally, for 25–30 minutes, or until the turkey is cooked through and tender.

4 Preheat the broiler to medium. Stir the cannellini beans into the casserole. Simmer for an additional 5 minutes. Sprinkle the breadcrumbs over the top and place under the preheated broiler for 2–3 minutes, or until golden. Serve, garnished with basil sprigs.

duck legs with olives

ingredients

SERVES 4

4 duck legs, all visible fat trimmed off

1 lb 12 oz/800 g canned chopped tomatoes

8 garlic cloves, peeled, but left whole

1 large onion, chopped

1 carrot, peeled and finely chopped

1 celery stalk, peeled and finely chopped

3 fresh thyme sprigs

generous $^1/_2$ cup Spanish green olives in brine, stuffed with pimientos, garlic, or almonds, drained and rinsed

1 tsp finely grated orange rind

salt and pepper

method

1 Put the duck legs in the bottom of a flameproof casserole or a large heavy-bottom skillet with a tight-fitting lid. Add the tomatoes, garlic, onion, carrot, celery, thyme, and olives and stir together. Season to taste with salt and pepper.

2 Turn the heat to high and cook, uncovered, until the ingredients start to bubble. Reduce the heat to low, cover tightly, and let simmer for $1^1/_4$–$1^1/_2$ hours, until the duck is very tender. Check occasionally and add a little water if the mixture appears to be drying out.

3 When the duck is tender, transfer it to a serving platter, cover, and keep hot. Leave the casserole uncovered, increase the heat to medium, and cook, stirring, for about 10 minutes, until the mixture forms a sauce. Stir in the orange rind, then taste and adjust the seasoning, adding salt and pepper if necessary.

4 Mash the tender garlic cloves with a fork and spread over the duck legs. Spoon the sauce over the top. Serve immediately.

duck jambalaya-style stew

ingredients

SERVES 4

4 duck breasts, about
    $5^1/2$ oz/150 g each

2 tbsp olive oil

8 oz/225 g piece ham,
    cut into small chunks

8 oz/225 g chorizo, outer
    casing removed

1 onion, chopped

3 garlic cloves, chopped

3 celery stalks, chopped

1–2 fresh red chiles, seeded
    and chopped

1 green bell pepper, seeded
    and chopped

$2^1/2$ cups chicken stock

1 tbsp chopped fresh oregano

14 oz/400 g canned chopped
    tomatoes

1–2 tsp hot pepper sauce,
    or to taste

chopped fresh parsley,
    to garnish

salad greens and freshly
    cooked rice, to serve

method

1 Remove and discard the skin and any fat from the duck breasts. Cut the flesh into bite-size pieces.

2 Heat half the oil in a large deep skillet and cook the duck, ham, and chorizo over high heat, stirring frequently, for 5 minutes, or until browned on all sides and sealed. Using a slotted spoon, remove from the skillet and set aside.

3 Add the onion, garlic, celery, and chiles to the skillet and cook over medium heat, stirring frequently, for 5 minutes, or until softened. Add the green bell pepper, then stir in the stock, oregano, tomatoes, and hot pepper sauce.

4 Bring to a boil, then reduce the heat and return the duck, ham, and chorizo to the skillet. Cover and simmer, stirring occasionally, for 20 minutes, or until the duck and ham are tender.

5 Serve immediately, garnished with parsley and accompanied by salad greens and rice.

fish & seafood

Virtually every country with a coastline boasts its own fish and seafood specialty and, more often than not, this will be a one-pot dish. Yet they are all distinctive, whether a hot Indian biryani with succulent shrimp nestling in golden fluffy rice, a colorful Spanish stew of mixed fish and shellfish, or a subtly spiced Moroccan tagine redolent with the fragrances of lemon and cilantro. Cooks worldwide have all reached the same conclusion—that where fish is concerned, more is often best. In this context, more implies a wealth of complementary ingredients cooked with the fish or, very frequently, a medley of fish and shellfish.

As well as stews, curries, and risottos, one-pot fish dishes may be roasted, broiled, poached, or baked in parcels. Roasted fish and seafood are a sensational taste revelation and are certainly special enough to serve to guests, while seafood parcels are both easy to prepare and fun to serve. Besides this range of cooking techniques, there is also a great choice of fish and seafood with different flavors, textures, and colors. Nutritionists recommend that we should eat fish at least twice a week and, with this choice of delicious, easy, and varied one-pot dishes, that couldn't be easier.

spanish seafood stew

ingredients

SERVES 4–6

large pinch of saffron threads

4 tbsp almost-boiling water

6 tbsp olive oil

1 large onion, chopped

2 garlic cloves, finely
chopped

1½ tbsp chopped fresh
thyme leaves

2 bay leaves

2 red bell peppers, seeded
and coarsely chopped

1 lb 12 oz/800 g canned
chopped tomatoes

1 tsp smoked paprika

1 cup fish stock

1 cup blanched almonds,
toasted and finely ground

12–16 mussels, scrubbed
and debearded

12–16 clams, scrubbed

1 lb 5 oz/600 g thick boneless
hake or cod fillets, skinned
and cut into 2-inch/5-cm
chunks

12–16 raw shrimp, peeled
and deveined

salt and pepper

crusty bread, to serve

method

1 Put the saffron threads in a heatproof pitcher with the water and let stand for at least 10 minutes to steep.

2 Heat the oil in a large heavy-bottom flameproof casserole over medium–high heat. Reduce the heat to low and cook the onion, stirring occasionally, for 10 minutes, or until golden but not browned. Stir in the garlic, thyme, bay leaves, and bell peppers and cook, stirring frequently, for 5 minutes, or until the bell peppers have softened.

3 Add the tomatoes and paprika and simmer, stirring frequently, for an additional 5 minutes.

4 Stir in the stock, the saffron and its soaking liquid, and the almonds and bring to a boil, stirring. Reduce the heat and simmer for 5–10 minutes, or until the sauce reduces and thickens. Season to taste with salt and pepper.

5 Meanwhile, discard any mussels and clams with broken shells and any that refuse to close when tapped.

6 Gently stir the fish into the stew, then add the shrimp, mussels, and clams. Reduce the heat to very low, then cover and simmer for 5 minutes, or until the fish is opaque, the mussels and clams have opened, and the shrimp have turned pink. Discard any mussels or clams that remain closed. Serve immediately with crusty bread.

squid with parsley & pine nuts

ingredients

SERVES 4

1/2 cup golden raisins

5 tbsp olive oil

2 tbsp chopped fresh flat-leaf
   parsley, plus extra
   to garnish

2 garlic cloves, finely
   chopped

1 lb 12 oz/800 g prepared
   squid, sliced, or squid
   rings

1/2 cup dry white wine

1 lb 2 oz/500 g strained
   tomatoes

pinch of chili powder

3/4 cup pine nuts, finely
   chopped

salt

method

1 Place the golden raisins in a small bowl, cover with lukewarm water, and set aside for 15 minutes to plump up.

2 Meanwhile, heat the oil in a heavy-bottom pan. Add the parsley and garlic and cook over low heat, stirring frequently, for 3 minutes. Add the squid and cook, stirring occasionally, for 5 minutes.

3 Increase the heat to medium, pour in the wine, and cook until it has almost completely evaporated. Stir in the strained tomatoes and season to taste with chili powder and salt. Reduce the heat again, cover, and let simmer gently, stirring occasionally, for 45–50 minutes, until the squid is almost tender.

4 Drain the golden raisins and stir them into the pan with the pine nuts. Let simmer for an additional 10 minutes, then serve immediately, garnished with chopped parsley.

seafood in saffron sauce

ingredients

SERVES 4

8 oz/225 g mussels

8 oz/225 g clams

2 tbsp olive oil

1 onion, sliced

pinch of saffron threads

1 tbsp chopped fresh thyme

2 garlic cloves, finely
    chopped

1 lb 12 oz/800 g canned
    tomatoes, drained and
    chopped

³/₄ cup dry white wine

8 cups fish stock

12 oz/350 g red snapper
    fillets, cut into bite-size
    chunks

1 lb/450 g monkfish fillet,
    cut into bite-size chunks

8 oz/225 g raw squid rings

2 tbsp fresh shredded basil
    leaves

salt and pepper

crusty bread, to serve

method

1 Clean the mussels and clams by scrubbing or scraping the shells and pulling out any beards that are attached to the mussels. Discard any with broken shells and any that refuse to close when tapped.

2 Heat the oil in a large flameproof casserole and cook the onion with the saffron, thyme, and a pinch of salt over low heat, stirring occasionally, for 5 minutes, or until softened.

3 Add the garlic and cook, stirring, for 2 minutes. Add the tomatoes, wine, and stock, then season to taste with salt and pepper and stir well. Bring to a boil, then reduce the heat and simmer for 15 minutes.

4 Add the fish chunks and simmer for an additional 3 minutes. Add the clams, mussels, and squid rings and simmer for an additional 5 minutes, or until the mussels and clams have opened. Discard any that remain closed. Stir in the basil and serve immediately, accompanied by plenty of crusty bread to mop up the broth.

seafood stew with red wine & tomatoes

ingredients

SERVES 4–6

12 oz/350 g mussels,
  scrubbed and debearded
4 tbsp olive oil
1 onion, finely chopped
1 green bell pepper, seeded
  and chopped
2 garlic cloves, very finely
  chopped
5 tbsp tomato paste
1 tbsp chopped fresh flat-leaf
  parsley
1 tsp dried oregano
14 oz/400 g canned chopped
  tomatoes
1 cup dry red wine
1 lb/450 g firm whitefish, such
  as cod or monkfish, cut
  into 2-inch/5-cm pieces
4 oz/115 g scallops, halved
4 oz/115 g raw shrimp,
  peeled and deveined
7 oz/200 g canned crabmeat
salt and pepper
10–15 fresh basil leaves,
  shredded, to garnish

method

1 Discard any mussels with broken shells and any that refuse to close when tapped.

2 Heat the oil in a large heavy-bottom pan or flameproof casserole over medium heat. Add the onion and bell pepper and cook for 5 minutes, or until beginning to soften.

3 Stir in the garlic, tomato paste, parsley, and oregano and cook for 1 minute, stirring. Pour in the tomatoes and wine. Season to taste with salt and pepper.

4 Bring to a boil, then cover and simmer over low heat for 30 minutes. Add the fish, cover, and simmer for 15 minutes.

5 Add the mussels, scallops, shrimp, and crabmeat. Cover and cook for an additional 15 minutes. Discard any mussels that remain closed. Stir in the basil just before serving.

moroccan fish tagine

ingredients

SERVES 4

2 tbsp olive oil

1 large onion, finely chopped

pinch of saffron threads

$^1/_2$ tsp ground cinnamon

1 tsp ground coriander

$^1/_2$ tsp ground cumin

$^1/_2$ tsp ground turmeric

7 oz/200 g canned chopped
   tomatoes

1$^1/_4$ cups fish stock

4 small red snappers,
   cleaned, boned, and
   heads and tails removed

2 oz/55 g pitted green olives

1 tbsp chopped preserved
   lemon

3 tbsp chopped fresh cilantro

salt and pepper

freshly cooked couscous,
   to serve

method

1 Heat the oil in a flameproof casserole. Add the onion and cook gently over very low heat, stirring occasionally, for 10 minutes, or until softened but not colored. Add the saffron, cinnamon, ground coriander, cumin, and turmeric and cook for an additional 30 seconds, stirring constantly.

2 Add the tomatoes and stock and stir well. Bring to a boil, reduce the heat, cover, and simmer for 15 minutes. Uncover and simmer for 20–35 minutes, or until thickened.

3 Cut each red snapper in half, then add the fish pieces to the casserole, pushing them down into the liquid. Simmer the stew for an additional 5–6 minutes, or until the fish is just cooked.

4 Carefully stir in the olives, lemon, and fresh cilantro. Season to taste with salt and pepper and serve immediately with couscous.

seafood chili

ingredients

SERVES 4

4 oz/115 g raw shrimp, peeled
and deveined

9 oz/250 g prepared scallops,
thawed if frozen

4 oz/115 g monkfish fillet,
cut into chunks

1 lime, peeled and thinly sliced

1 tbsp chili powder

1 tsp ground cumin

3 tbsp chopped fresh cilantro

2 garlic cloves, finely chopped

1 fresh green chile, seeded
and chopped

3 tbsp corn oil

1 onion, coarsely chopped

1 red bell pepper, seeded and
coarsely chopped

1 yellow bell pepper, seeded
and coarsely chopped

$1/4$ tsp ground cloves

pinch of ground cinnamon

pinch of cayenne pepper

$1^1/2$ cups fish stock

14 oz/400 g canned chopped
tomatoes

14 oz/400 g canned red
kidney beans, drained
and rinsed

salt

method

1 Place the shrimp, scallops, monkfish, and lime in a large nonmetallic dish with $1/4$ teaspoon of the chili powder, $1/4$ teaspoon of the ground cumin, 1 tablespoon of the chopped cilantro, half the garlic, the fresh chile, and 1 tablespoon of the oil. Cover with plastic wrap and let marinate for up to 1 hour.

2 Meanwhile, heat 1 tablespoon of the remaining oil in a flameproof casserole or large heavy-bottom pan. Add the onion, the remaining garlic, and the red and yellow bell peppers and cook over low heat, stirring occasionally, for 5 minutes, or until softened.

3 Add the remaining chili powder, the remaining cumin, the cloves, cinnamon, and cayenne with the remaining oil, if necessary, and season to taste with salt. Cook, stirring, for 5 minutes, then gradually stir in the stock and the tomatoes with their juices. Partially cover and simmer for 25 minutes.

4 Add the beans to the tomato mixture and spoon the fish and shellfish on top. Cover and cook for 10 minutes, or until the fish and shellfish are cooked through. Sprinkle with the remaining cilantro and serve.

mediterranean fish stew

ingredients

SERVES 4

2 tbsp olive oil

1 onion, sliced

pinch of saffron threads,
    lightly crushed

1 tbsp chopped fresh thyme

2 garlic cloves, finely
    chopped

1 lb 12 oz/800 g canned
    chopped tomatoes,
    drained

8 cups fish stock

3/4 cup dry white wine

12 oz/350 g red snapper
    or pompano fillets,
    cut into chunks

1 lb/450 g monkfish fillet,
    cut into chunks

1 lb/450 g clams, scrubbed

8 oz/225 g squid rings

2 tbsp fresh basil leaves,
    plus extra to garnish

salt and pepper

method

1 Heat the oil in a large flameproof casserole. Add the onion, saffron, thyme, and a pinch of salt. Cook over low heat, stirring occasionally, for 5 minutes, or until the onion has softened.

2 Add the garlic and cook for an additional 2 minutes, then add the drained tomatoes and pour in the stock and wine. Season to taste with salt and pepper, bring the mixture to a boil, then reduce the heat and simmer for 15 minutes.

3 Add the chunks of red snapper and monkfish and simmer for 3 minutes.

4 Discard any clams with broken shells and any that refuse to close when tapped. Add the remaining clams and squid to the casserole and simmer for 5 minutes, or until the clam shells have opened.

5 Discard any clams that remain closed. Tear in the basil and stir. Serve garnished with the basil leaves.

italian fish stew

ingredients

SERVES 4

2 tbsp olive oil

2 red onions, finely chopped

1 garlic clove, crushed

2 zucchini, sliced

14 oz/400 g canned chopped
  tomatoes

3³/₄ cups fish stock or
  vegetable stock

³/₄ cup dried pasta shapes

12 oz/350 g firm whitefish,
  such as cod or hake

1 tbsp chopped fresh basil,
  plus extra sprigs to garnish

1 tsp grated lemon rind

1 tbsp cornstarch

1 tbsp water

salt and pepper

method

1 Heat the oil in a large pan. Add the onions and garlic and cook over low heat, stirring occasionally, for about 5 minutes, until softened. Add the zucchini and cook, stirring frequently, for 2–3 minutes.

2 Add the tomatoes and stock to the pan and bring to a boil. Add the pasta, bring back to a boil, reduce the heat, and cover. Simmer for 5 minutes.

3 Skin and bone the fish, then cut it into chunks. Add to the pan with the basil and lemon rind and simmer gently for 5 minutes, until the fish is opaque and flakes easily (be careful to avoid overcooking it) and the pasta is tender, but still firm to the bite.

4 Place the cornstarch and water in a small bowl, mix to a smooth paste, and stir into the stew. Cook gently for 2 minutes, stirring constantly, until thickened. Season to taste with salt and pepper.

5 Ladle the stew into 4 warmed bowls. Garnish with basil and serve immediately.

moules marinières

ingredients

SERVES 4

4 lb 8 oz/2 kg mussels

1¹/₄ cups dry white wine

6 shallots, finely chopped

1 bouquet garni

pepper

4 bay leaves, to garnish

crusty bread, to serve

method

1 Clean the mussels by scrubbing or scraping the shells and pulling off any beards. Discard any with broken shells and any that refuse to close when tapped with a knife. Rinse the mussels under cold running water.

2 Pour the wine into a large heavy-bottom pan, add the shallots and bouquet garni, and season to taste with pepper. Bring to a boil over medium heat. Add the mussels, cover tightly, and cook, shaking the pan occasionally, for 5 minutes.

3 Remove and discard the bouquet garni and any mussels that remain closed. Divide the mussels among 4 soup plates with a slotted spoon. Tilt the casserole to let any sand settle, then spoon the cooking liquid over the mussels. Garnish with bay leaves and serve immediately with crusty bread.

roasted seafood

ingredients

SERVES 4

1 lb 5 oz/600 g new potatoes,
   halved if large, parboiled

3 red onions, cut into wedges

2 zucchini, cut into chunks

8 garlic cloves, peeled but
   left whole

2 lemons, cut into wedges

4 fresh rosemary sprigs

4 tbsp olive oil

12 oz/350 g unpeeled raw
   shrimp

2 small squid, cut into rings

4 tomatoes, quartered

method

1 Preheat the oven to 400°F/200°C. Place the potatoes in a large roasting pan together with the onions, zucchini, garlic, lemons, and rosemary sprigs.

2 Pour over the oil and toss to coat all the vegetables in it. Roast in the preheated oven for 30 minutes, turning occasionally, until the potatoes are tender.

3 Once the potatoes are tender, add the shrimp, squid, and tomatoes, tossing to coat them in the oil, and roast for 10 minutes. All the vegetables should be cooked through and slightly charred for full flavor.

4 Transfer the roasted seafood and vegetables to warmed serving plates and serve hot.

goan-style seafood curry

ingredients

SERVES 4–6

3 tbsp vegetable oil or
    peanut oil
1 tbsp black mustard seeds
12 fresh or 1 tbsp dried
    curry leaves
6 shallots, finely chopped
1 garlic clove, crushed
1 tsp ground turmeric
$1/2$ tsp ground coriander
$1/4$–$1/2$ tsp chili powder
scant 3 cups coconut cream
1 lb 2 oz/500 g skinless,
    boneless whitefish, such
    as monkfish or cod, cut
    into large chunks
1 lb/450 g large raw shrimp,
    peeled and deveined
juice and finely grated rind
    of 1 lime
salt
lime wedges, to serve

method

1 Heat the oil in a wok or large skillet over high heat. Add the mustard seeds and stir them around for about 1 minute, or until they jump. Stir in the curry leaves.

2 Add the shallots and garlic and stir for about 5 minutes, or until the shallots are golden. Stir in the turmeric, coriander, and chili powder and continue stirring for about 30 seconds.

3 Add the coconut cream. Bring to a boil, then reduce the heat to medium and stir for about 2 minutes.

4 Reduce the heat to low, add the fish, and simmer for 1 minute, spooning the sauce over the fish and very gently spooning it around. Add the shrimp and continue to simmer for an additional 4–5 minutes, until the fish flesh flakes easily and the shrimp turn pink and curl.

5 Add half the lime juice, then taste and add more lime juice and salt to taste. Sprinkle with the lime rind and serve with lime wedges.

jambalaya

ingredients

SERVES 4

2 tbsp vegetable oil

2 onions, coarsely chopped

1 green bell pepper, seeded
and coarsely chopped

2 celery stalks, coarsely
chopped

3 garlic cloves, finely chopped

2 tsp paprika

$10^1/2$ oz/300 g skinless,
boneless chicken breasts,
chopped

$3^1/2$ oz/100 g boudin
sausages, chopped

3 tomatoes, peeled and
chopped

2 cups long-grain rice

$3^3/4$ cups chicken stock
or fish stock

1 tsp dried oregano

2 bay leaves

12 large jumbo shrimp,
peeled and deveined

4 scallions, finely chopped

2 tbsp chopped fresh parsley,
plus extra to garnish

salt and pepper

method

1 Heat the oil in a large skillet over low heat. Add the onions, bell pepper, celery, and garlic and cook for 8–10 minutes, until all the vegetables have softened.

2 Add the paprika and cook for another 30 seconds. Add the chicken and sausages and cook for 8–10 minutes, until lightly browned. Add the tomatoes and cook for 2–3 minutes, until they have collapsed.

3 Add the rice to the pan and stir well. Pour in the stock, oregano, and bay leaves and stir well. Cover and let simmer for 10 minutes.

4 Add the shrimp and stir well. Cover again and cook for another 6–8 minutes, until the rice is tender and the shrimp are cooked through.

5 Stir in the scallions and parsley, and season to taste with salt and pepper. Transfer to a large serving dish, garnish with chopped parsley, and serve.

shrimp with coconut rice

ingredients

SERVES 4

1 cup dried Chinese
   mushrooms
1 tbsp vegetable oil or
   peanut oil
6 scallions, chopped
scant 1/2 cup dry
   unsweetened coconut
1 fresh green chile, seeded
   and chopped
generous 1 cup jasmine rice
2/3 cup fish stock
13/4 cups coconut milk
12 oz/350 g cooked, peeled
   shrimp
6 fresh Thai basil sprigs

method

1 Place the mushrooms in a small bowl, cover with hot water, and set aside to soak for 30 minutes. Drain, then cut off and discard the stalks and slice the caps.

2 Heat the oil in a wok and stir-fry the scallions, coconut, and chile for 2–3 minutes, until lightly browned. Add the mushrooms and stir-fry for 3–4 minutes.

3 Add the rice and stir-fry for 2–3 minutes, then add the stock and bring to a boil. Reduce the heat and add the coconut milk. Let simmer for 10–15 minutes, until the rice is tender. Stir in the shrimp and basil, heat through, and serve.

shrimp biryani

ingredients

SERVES 4

1 tsp saffron threads

4 tbsp lukewarm water

2 shallots, coarsely chopped

3 garlic cloves, crushed

1 tsp chopped fresh ginger

2 tsp coriander seeds

1/2 tsp black peppercorns

2 cloves

seeds from 2 green
    cardamom pods

1-inch/2.5-cm piece
    cinnamon stick

1 tsp ground turmeric

1 fresh green chile, chopped

1/2 tsp salt

2 tbsp ghee

1 tsp black mustard seeds

14 oz/400 g raw jumbo
    shrimp, peeled and
    deveined

1 1/4 cups coconut milk

1 1/4 cups lowfat plain yogurt

freshly cooked rice, to serve

to garnish

toasted slivered almonds

1 scallion, sliced

fresh cilantro sprigs

method

1 Soak the saffron in the lukewarm water for
10 minutes. Put the shallots, garlic, spices,
chile, and salt into a spice grinder or mortar
and grind to a paste.

2 Heat the ghee in a saucepan and add
the mustard seeds. When they start to pop,
add the shrimp and stir over a high heat for
1 minute. Stir in the spice mix, then the coconut
milk and yogurt. Simmer for 20 minutes.

3 Spoon the shrimp mixture into serving
bowls. Top with the freshly cooked rice and
drizzle over the saffron water. Serve garnished
with the slivered almonds, scallion slices,
and cilantro sprigs.

shrimp & chicken paella

ingredients

SERVES 6–8

16 mussels, scrubbed and
   debearded

$1/2$ tsp saffron threads

2 tbsp hot water

generous $1^3/4$ cups
   medium-grain paella rice

6 tbsp olive oil

6–8 unboned, skin-on
   chicken thighs, excess fat
   removed

5 oz/140 g Spanish chorizo
   sausage, casing removed,
   cut into $1/4$-inch/5-mm
   slices

2 large onions, chopped

4 large garlic cloves, crushed

1 tsp mild or hot Spanish
   paprika, to taste

$3^1/2$ oz/100 g green beans,
   chopped

generous $3/4$ cup frozen peas

5 cups fish stock, chicken
   stock, or vegetable stock

16 raw shrimp, peeled and
   deveined

2 red bell peppers, halved
   and seeded, then broiled,
   peeled, and sliced

salt and pepper

3 tbsp chopped fresh parsley,
   to garnish

method

1 Discard any mussels with broken shells and any that refuse to close when tapped. Put the saffron threads and hot water in a bowl and let steep. Meanwhile, put the rice in a strainer and rinse in cold water.

2 Heat half the oil in a paella pan or ovenproof casserole. Cook the chicken over medium–high heat, turning frequently, for 5 minutes, or until golden. Transfer to a bowl. Add the chorizo to the pan and cook, stirring, for 1 minute, or until beginning to crisp. Add to the chicken.

3 Heat the remaining oil in the pan and cook the onions for 2 minutes. Add the garlic and paprika and cook for an additional 3 minutes.

4 Add the drained rice, beans, and peas and stir until coated in oil. Return the chicken, chorizo, and any juices to the pan. Stir in the stock, saffron and its soaking liquid, and salt and pepper to taste and bring to a boil, stirring constantly. Reduce the heat to low and let simmer, uncovered and without stirring, for 15 minutes, or until the rice is almost tender and most of the liquid has been absorbed.

5 Arrange the mussels, shrimp, and bell peppers on top, then cover and simmer, without stirring, for an additional 5 minutes, or until the shrimp turn pink and the mussels open. Discard any mussels that remain closed. Sprinkle with the parsley and serve.

seafood risotto

ingredients

SERVES 4

1 tbsp olive oil

4 tbsp butter

2 garlic cloves, chopped

1³/₄ cups risotto rice

generous 5¹/₂ cups boiling
    fish stock or chicken stock

9 oz/250 g mixed cooked
    seafood, such as shrimp,
    squid, mussels, and clams

2 tbsp chopped fresh
    oregano, plus extra
    to garnish

¹/₂ cup freshly grated
    Parmesan cheese

salt and pepper

method

1 Heat the oil with 2 tablespoons of the butter in a deep pan over medium heat until the butter has melted. Add the garlic and cook, stirring, for 1 minute.

2 Reduce the heat, add the rice, and mix to coat in oil and butter. Cook, stirring constantly, for 2–3 minutes, or until the grains are translucent.

3 Gradually add the hot stock, a ladleful at a time. Stir constantly and add more liquid as the rice absorbs each addition. Increase the heat to medium so that the liquid bubbles. Cook for 20 minutes, or until all the liquid is absorbed and the rice is creamy.

4 About 5 minutes before the rice is ready, add the seafood and oregano to the pan and mix well.

5 Remove the pan from the heat and season to taste with salt and pepper. Add the remaining butter and mix well, then stir in the grated cheese until it melts. Spoon onto warmed plates and serve immediately, garnished with oregano.

spicy tuna with fennel & onions

ingredients

SERVES 4

4 tuna steaks, about 5 oz/
    140 g each
2 fennel bulbs, thickly sliced
    lengthwise
2 red onions, sliced
2 tbsp extra virgin olive oil

marinade
$^1/_2$ cup extra virgin olive oil
4 garlic cloves, finely chopped
4 fresh red chiles, seeded
    and finely chopped
juice and finely grated rind of
    2 lemons
4 tbsp finely chopped fresh
    flat-leaf parsley
salt and pepper

method

1 Whisk all the marinade ingredients together in a small bowl. Put the tuna steaks in a large shallow dish and spoon over 4 tablespoons of the marinade, turning until well coated. Cover and let marinate in the refrigerator for 30 minutes. Set aside the remaining marinade.

2 Heat a grill pan over high heat. Put the fennel and onions in a separate bowl, add the oil, and toss well to coat. Add to the grill pan and cook for 5 minutes on each side, until just beginning to color. Transfer to 4 warmed serving plates, drizzle with the reserved marinade, and keep warm.

3 Add the tuna steaks to the grill pan and cook, turning once, for 4–5 minutes, until firm to the touch but still moist inside. Transfer the tuna to the serving plates and serve immediately.

swordfish with tomatoes & olives

ingredients

SERVES 4

2 tbsp olive oil

1 onion, finely chopped

1 celery stalk, finely chopped

4 oz/115 g green olives, pitted

1 lb/450 g tomatoes, chopped

3 tbsp bottled capers, drained

4 swordfish steaks, about
     5 oz/140 g each

salt and pepper

fresh flat-leaf parsley sprigs,
     to garnish

method

1 Heat the oil in a large heavy-bottom pan. Add the onion and celery and cook over low heat, stirring occasionally, for 5 minutes, or until softened.

2 Meanwhile, coarsely chop half the olives. Stir the chopped and whole olives into the pan with the tomatoes and capers, then season to taste with salt and pepper.

3 Bring to a boil, then reduce the heat, cover, and simmer gently, stirring occasionally, for 15 minutes.

4 Add the swordfish steaks to the pan and return to a boil. Cover and simmer for 20 minutes, or until the fish is cooked and the flesh flakes easily, turning the fish once during cooking. Transfer the fish to serving plates and spoon over the sauce. Garnish with parsley and serve immediately.

monkfish parcels

ingredients

SERVES 4

4 tsp olive oil

2 zucchini, sliced

1 large red bell pepper, peeled,
seeded, and cut into strips

2 monkfish fillets, about
4^{1}/$_{2}$ oz/125 g each, skin
and membrane removed

6 smoked lean bacon strips

salt and pepper

freshly cooked pasta and
slices of olive bread,
to serve

method

1 Preheat the oven to 375°F/190°C. Cut
4 large pieces of foil, about 9 inches/23 cm
square. Brush lightly with a little of the oil,
then divide the zucchini and bell pepper
among them.

2 Rinse the fish fillets under cold running water
and pat dry with paper towels. Cut them in
half, then put 1 piece on top of each pile of
zucchini and bell pepper. Cut the bacon strips
in half and lay 3 pieces across each piece of
fish. Season to taste with salt and pepper,
drizzle over the remaining oil, and close up
the parcels. Seal tightly, transfer to an
ovenproof dish, and bake in the preheated
oven for 25 minutes.

3 Remove from the oven, open each foil parcel
slightly, and serve with pasta and slices of
olive bread.

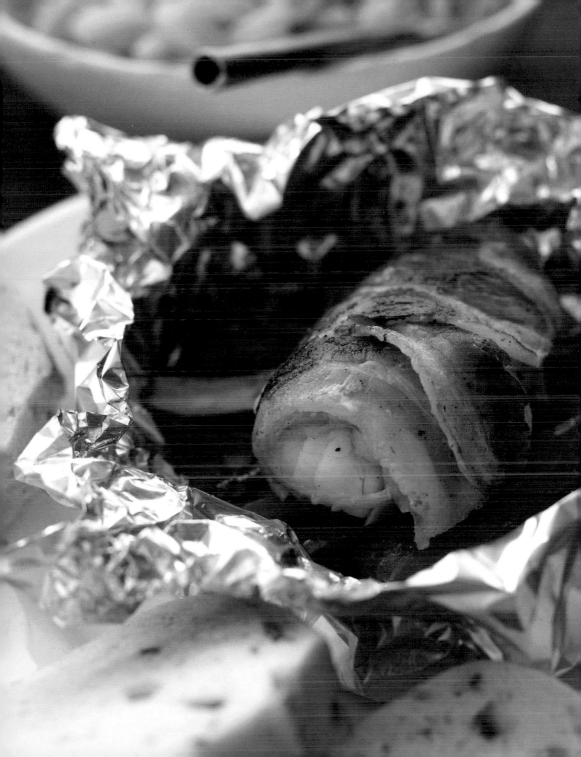

spicy monkfish rice

ingredients

SERVES 4

1 hot red chile, seeded and
    chopped

1 tsp chile flakes

2 garlic cloves, chopped

2 pinches of saffron

3 tbsp coarsely chopped mint
    leaves, plus extra
    to garnish

4 tbsp olive oil

2 tbsp lemon juice

12 oz/350 g monkfish fillet,
    cut into bite-size pieces

1 onion, finely chopped

1 cup long-grain rice

14 oz/400 g canned chopped
    tomatoes

3/4 cup coconut milk

1 cup peas

salt and pepper

method

1 In a food processor or blender, blend the fresh and dried chile, garlic, saffron, mint, oil, and lemon juice until finely chopped but not smooth.

2 Put the monkfish into a nonmetallic dish and pour over the spice paste, mixing together well. Set aside for 20 minutes to marinate.

3 Heat a large pan until it is very hot. Using a slotted spoon, lift the monkfish from the marinade and add, in batches, to the hot pan. Cook for 3–4 minutes, until browned and firm. Remove with a slotted spoon and set aside.

4 Add the onion and remaining marinade to the same pan and cook for 5 minutes, until softened and lightly browned. Add the rice and stir until well coated. Add the tomatoes and coconut milk. Bring to a boil, cover, and simmer very gently for 15 minutes.

5 Stir in the peas, season to taste with salt and pepper, and arrange the fish over the top. Cover and continue to cook over very low heat for 5 minutes. Serve garnished with the chopped mint.

vegetables &
beans

It could be said that vegetables are the perfect choice for one-pot cooking because there is such a enormous variety and they go so well together. They're also great combined with beans, providing a well-balanced, healthy, and, of course, flavorsome meal. Whether you're using fresh-tasting baby vegetables in the spring, filling and satisfying roots in the winter, or the sun-ripened harvest of the summer, the options are almost endless and there is sure to be a dish to suit everyone. Even those who claim not to like vegetables will be pleasantly surprised by how delicious they are when they are cooked together in a mouthwatering one-pot medley.

Vegetarian stews and casseroles can be either warming and substantial or more delicate and subtle, and have the added advantage of requiring less cooking time than their meat-based counterparts. Other one-pot techniques are usually even quicker and vegetables are great stir-fried, roasted, and baked, as well as combined in curries, risottos, and pilafs. With these tasty options, you not only save time but money, too, because they are very economical. There's every reason to include a one-pot vegetarian dish in the family menu occasionally, even if you eat meat the rest of the time. Whichever recipe you choose, eating more vegetables has never been more enjoyable.

italian vegetable stew

ingredients

SERVES 4

4 garlic cloves

1 small acorn squash, seeded
    and peeled

1 red onion, sliced

2 leeks, sliced

1 eggplant, sliced

1 small celery root, diced

2 turnips, sliced

2 plum tomatoes, chopped

1 carrot, sliced

1 zucchini, sliced

2 red bell peppers, seeded
    and chopped

1 fennel bulb, sliced

6 oz/175 g Swiss chard,
    chopped

2 bay leaves

$^1/_2$ tsp fennel seeds

$^1/_2$ tsp chili powder

pinch each of dried thyme,
    dried oregano, and sugar

$^1/_2$ cup extra virgin olive oil

scant 1 cup vegetable stock

1 oz/25 g fresh basil leaves,
    torn

4 tbsp chopped fresh parsley

salt and pepper

2 tbsp freshly grated
    Parmesan cheese,
    to serve

method

1 Finely chop the garlic and dice the squash. Put them in a large heavy-bottom pan with a tight-fitting lid. Add the onion, leeks, eggplant, celery root, turnips, tomatoes, carrot, zucchini, red bell peppers, fennel, Swiss chard, bay leaves, fennel seeds, chili powder, thyme, oregano, sugar, oil, stock, and half the basil to the pan. Mix together well, then bring to a boil.

2 Reduce the heat, then cover and simmer for 30 minutes, or until all the vegetables are tender.

3 Sprinkle in the remaining basil and the parsley and season to taste with salt and pepper. Serve immediately, sprinkled with the cheese.

spring stew

ingredients

SERVES 4

2 tbsp olive oil

4–8 pearl onions, halved

2 celery stalks, cut into
$^{1}/_{4}$-inch/5-mm slices

8 oz/225 g baby carrots,
scrubbed and halved
if large

10$^{1}/_{2}$ oz/300 g new potatoes,
scrubbed and halved,
or cut into quarters if large

3$^{3}/_{4}$–5 cups vegetable stock

generous 2$^{3}/_{4}$ cups canned
cannellini beans, drained
and rinsed

1 fresh bouquet garni

1$^{1}/_{2}$–2 tbsp light soy sauce

3 oz/85 g baby corn

1 cup frozen or shelled fresh
fava beans, thawed
if frozen

$^{1}/_{2}$–1 head of savoy or spring
cabbage, about 8 oz/225 g

1$^{1}/_{2}$ tbsp cornstarch

2 tbsp cold water

salt and pepper

$^{1}/_{2}$–$^{3}/_{4}$ cup grated Parmesan
or sharp cheddar cheese,
to serve

method

1 Heat the oil in a large heavy-bottom pan with a tight-fitting lid, and cook the onions, celery, carrots, and potatoes, stirring frequently, for 5 minutes, or until softened. Add the stock, drained beans, bouquet garni, and soy sauce, then bring to a boil. Reduce the heat, then cover and simmer for 12 minutes.

2 Add the baby corn and fava beans and season to taste with salt and pepper. Simmer for an additional 3 minutes.

3 Meanwhile, discard the outer leaves and hard central core from the cabbage and shred the leaves. Add to the pan and simmer for an additional 3–5 minutes, or until all the vegetables are tender.

4 Blend the cornstarch with the water, then stir into the pan and cook, stirring, for 4–6 minutes, or until the liquid has thickened. Serve the cheese separately, for stirring into the stew.

tuscan bean stew

ingredients

SERVES 4

1 large fennel bulb

2 tbsp olive oil

1 red onion, cut into small
  wedges

2–4 garlic cloves, sliced

1 fresh green chile, seeded
  and chopped

1 small eggplant, about
  8 oz/225 g, cut into chunks

2 tbsp tomato paste

scant 2–2$\frac{1}{2}$ cups vegetable
  stock

1 lb/450 g ripe tomatoes,
  chopped

1 tbsp balsamic vinegar

a few fresh oregano sprigs

14 oz/400 g canned
  cranberry beans

14 oz/400 g canned flageolets

1 yellow bell pepper, seeded
  and cut into small strips

1 zucchini, sliced into half
  moons

$\frac{1}{3}$ cup pitted black olives

$\frac{1}{4}$ cup fresh Parmesan
  cheese shavings

salt and pepper

crusty bread, to serve

method

1 Trim the fennel and reserve any feathery fronds, then cut the bulb into small strips. Heat the oil in a large heavy-bottom pan with a tight-fitting lid and cook the onion, garlic, chile, and fennel strips, stirring frequently, for 5–8 minutes, or until softened.

2 Add the eggplant and cook, stirring frequently, for 5 minutes. Blend the tomato paste with a little of the stock in a pitcher and pour over the fennel mixture, then add the remaining stock, the tomatoes, vinegar, and oregano. Bring to a boil, then reduce the heat and simmer, covered, for 15 minutes, or until the tomatoes have begun to collapse.

3 Drain and rinse the beans, then drain again. Add them to the pan with the bell pepper, zucchini, and olives. Simmer for an additional 15 minutes, or until the vegetables are tender. Taste and adjust the seasoning. Scatter over the Parmesan shavings and serve garnished with the reserved fennel fronds and accompanied by crusty bread.

potato & lemon casserole

ingredients

SERVES 4

scant $^1/_2$ cup olive oil

2 red onions, cut into
   8 wedges

3 garlic cloves, crushed

2 tsp ground cumin

2 tsp ground coriander

pinch of cayenne pepper

1 carrot, thickly sliced

2 small turnips, quartered

1 zucchini, sliced

1 lb 2 oz/500 g potatoes,
   thickly sliced

juice and grated rind of
   2 large lemons

$1^1/_4$ cups vegetable stock

2 tbsp chopped fresh cilantro

salt and pepper

method

1 Heat the oil in a flameproof casserole. Add the onions and sauté over medium heat, stirring frequently, for 3 minutes.

2 Add the garlic and cook for 30 seconds. Stir in the ground cumin, ground coriander, and cayenne and cook, stirring constantly, for 1 minute.

3 Add the carrot, turnips, zucchini, and potatoes and stir to coat in the oil.

4 Add the lemon juice and rind and the stock. Season to taste with salt and pepper. Cover and cook over medium heat, stirring occasionally, for 20–30 minutes, until tender.

5 Remove the lid, sprinkle in the chopped fresh cilantro, and stir well. Serve immediately.

lentil & rice casserole

ingredients

SERVES 4

1 cup red lentils

generous 1/4 cup long-grain
rice

5 cups vegetable stock

1 leek, cut into chunks

3 garlic cloves, crushed

14 oz/400 g canned chopped
tomatoes

1 tsp ground cumin

1 tsp chili powder

1 tsp garam masala

1 red bell pepper, seeded
and sliced

1 1/2 cups small broccoli
florets

8 baby corn, halved
lengthwise

2 oz/55 g green beans,
halved

1 tbsp shredded fresh basil,
plus extra sprigs to garnish

salt and pepper

method

1 Place the lentils, rice, and stock in a large flameproof casserole and cook over low heat, stirring occasionally, for 20 minutes.

2 Add the leek, garlic, tomatoes, ground cumin, chili powder, garam masala, bell pepper, broccoli, baby corn, and green beans to the casserole.

3 Bring the mixture to a boil, reduce the heat, cover, and simmer for an additional 10–15 minutes, or until all the vegetables are tender.

4 Add the shredded basil and season to taste with salt and pepper. Garnish with basil sprigs and serve immediately.

vegetable goulash

ingredients

SERVES 4

$1/4$ cup sun-dried tomatoes, chopped

2 tbsp olive oil

$1/2$–1 tsp crushed dried chiles

2–3 garlic cloves, chopped

1 large onion, cut into small wedges

1 small celery root, cut into small chunks

4 carrots, sliced

8 oz/225 g new potatoes, scrubbed and cut into chunks

1 small acorn squash, seeded, peeled, and cut into small chunks

2 tbsp tomato paste

$1^{1}/4$ cups vegetable stock

$2^{1}/2$ cups canned Puy or green lentils, drained and rinsed

1–2 tsp hot paprika

a few fresh thyme sprigs

1 lb/450 g ripe tomatoes

sour cream and crusty bread, to serve

method

1 Put the sun-dried tomatoes in a small heatproof bowl, then cover with almost-boiling water and let soak for 15–20 minutes. Drain, reserving the soaking liquid.

2 Heat the oil in a large heavy-bottom pan with a tight-fitting lid and cook the chiles, garlic, onion, celery root, carrots, potatoes, and squash, stirring frequently, for 5–8 minutes, or until softened.

3 Blend the tomato paste with a little of the stock in a pitcher and pour over the vegetable mixture, then add the remaining stock, lentils, the sun-dried tomatoes and their soaking liquid, the paprika, and thyme.

4 Bring to a boil, then reduce the heat and simmer, covered, for 15 minutes. Add the fresh tomatoes and simmer for an additional 15 minutes, or until the vegetables and lentils are tender. Serve topped with spoonfuls of sour cream and accompanied by crusty bread.

vegetable chili

ingredients

SERVES 4

1 medium eggplant, peeled
    if you want, cut into
    1-inch/2.5-cm slices

4 tsp olive oil

1 large red or yellow onion,
    finely chopped

2 red or yellow bell peppers,
    seeded and finely
    chopped

3–4 garlic cloves, finely
    chopped or crushed

1 lb 12 oz/800 g canned
    chopped tomatoes

1 tbsp mild chili powder,
    or to taste

1/2 tsp ground cumin

1/2 tsp dried oregano

2 small zucchini, quartered
    lengthwise and sliced

14 oz/400 g canned kidney
    beans, drained and rinsed

2 cups water

1 tbsp tomato paste

salt and pepper

finely chopped scallions and
    grated cheddar cheese,
    to serve

method

1 Brush the eggplant slices on one side with 1 teaspoon of the oil. Heat 1 teaspoon of the oil in a large heavy-bottom skillet over medium–high heat. Add the eggplant slices, oiled-side up, and cook for 5–6 minutes, until browned on one side. Turn the slices over, cook on the other side until browned, and then transfer to a plate. Cut the slices into bite-size pieces.

2 Heat the remaining oil in a large pan over medium heat. Add the onion and bell peppers and cook, stirring occasionally, for 3–4 minutes, until the onion is just softened but not browned. Add the garlic and continue cooking for 2–3 minutes, or until the onion is just beginning to color.

3 Add the tomatoes, chili powder, cumin, and oregano. Season to taste with salt and pepper. Bring just to a boil, reduce the heat, cover, and simmer gently for 15 minutes.

4 Add the zucchini, eggplant, and kidney beans. Stir in the water and tomato paste. Bring back to a boil, cover, and continue simmering for about 45 minutes, or until the vegetables are tender. Adjust the seasoning, adding salt and pepper if necessary. If you prefer a hotter dish, stir in a little more chili powder.

5 Ladle into warmed bowls and top with scallions and cheese.

spicy chickpea & eggplant casserole

ingredients

SERVES 6

1 tbsp cumin seeds

2 tbsp coriander seeds

2 tsp dried oregano or thyme

5 tbsp vegetable oil

2 onions, chopped

1 red bell pepper, seeded and
  cut into 3/4-inch/2-cm
  chunks

1 eggplant, cut into
  3/4-inch/2-cm chunks

2 garlic cloves, chopped

1 fresh green chile, chopped

14 oz/400 g canned chopped
  tomatoes

14 oz/400 g canned chickpeas,
  drained and rinsed

8 oz/225 g green beans, cut
  into 3/4-inch/2-cm lengths

2 1/2 cups stock

3 tbsp chopped fresh cilantro

method

1 Dry-roast the seeds in a heavy-bottom skillet for a few seconds, until aromatic. Add the oregano and cook for an additional few seconds. Remove from the heat, transfer to a mortar, and crush with a pestle.

2 Heat the oil in a large flameproof casserole dish. Cook the onions, bell pepper, and eggplant for 10 minutes, until softened. Add the ground seed mixture, garlic, and chile, and cook for an additional 2 minutes.

3 Add the tomatoes, chickpeas, green beans, and stock. Bring to a boil, then cover and simmer gently for 1 hour. Stir in the cilantro and serve immediately.

moroccan vegetable stew

ingredients

SERVES 4

2 tbsp olive oil

1 red onion, finely chopped

2–4 garlic cloves, crushed

1 fresh red chile, seeded and
    sliced

1 eggplant, about 8 oz/225 g,
    cut into small chunks

small piece fresh ginger,
    peeled and grated

1 tsp ground cumin

1 tsp ground coriander

pinch of saffron threads or
    $1/2$ tsp turmeric

1–2 cinnamon sticks

$1/2$–1 butternut squash, about
    1 lb/450 g, peeled, seeded,
    and cut into small chunks

1 large sweet potato, cut into
    small chunks

scant $1/2$ cup dried prunes

2–$2^1/2$ cups vegetable stock

4 tomatoes, chopped

14 oz/400 g canned
    chickpeas, drained
    and rinsed

1 tbsp chopped fresh cilantro,
    to garnish

method

1 Heat the oil in a large heavy-bottom pan with a tight-fitting lid, and cook the onion, garlic, chile, and eggplant, stirring frequently, for 5–8 minutes, or until softened.

2 Add the ginger, cumin, coriander, and saffron and cook, stirring constantly, for 2 minutes. Bruise the cinnamon stick.

3 Add the cinnamon stick, squash, sweet potato, prunes, stock, and tomatoes to the pan and bring to a boil. Reduce the heat, then cover and simmer, stirring occasionally, for 20 minutes. Add the chickpeas to the pan and cook for an additional 10 minutes. Discard the cinnamon stick and serve the stew garnished with the fresh cilantro.

chile bean stew

ingredients

SERVES 4–6

2 tbsp olive oil

1 onion, chopped

2–4 garlic cloves, chopped

2 fresh red chiles, seeded
and sliced

1²/₃ cups canned kidney
beans, drained and rinsed

1²/₃ cups canned cannellini
beans, drained and rinsed

1²/₃ cups canned chickpeas,
drained and rinsed

1 tbsp tomato paste

3–3³/₄ cups vegetable stock

1 red bell pepper, seeded
and chopped

4 tomatoes, coarsely chopped

1¹/₂ cups frozen or shelled
fresh fava beans, thawed
if frozen

1 tbsp chopped fresh cilantro,
plus extra to garnish

pepper

sour cream, to serve

pinch of paprika, to garnish

method

1 Heat the oil in a large heavy-bottom pan with a tight-fitting lid and cook the onion, garlic, and chiles, stirring frequently, for 5 minutes, or until softened. Add the kidney beans, cannellini beans, and chickpeas.

2 Blend the tomato paste with a little of the stock in a pitcher and pour over the bean mixture, then add the remaining stock. Bring to a boil, then reduce the heat and simmer for 10–15 minutes.

3 Add the bell pepper, tomatoes, fava beans, and pepper to taste and simmer for 15–20 minutes, or until all the vegetables are tender. Stir in the chopped cilantro.

4 Serve the stew topped with spoonfuls of sour cream and garnished with chopped cilantro and a pinch of paprika.

roast summer vegetables

ingredients

SERVES 4

1 fennel bulb, cut into wedges

2 red onions, cut into wedges

2 beefsteak tomatoes, cut
  into wedges

1 eggplant, thickly sliced

2 zucchini, thickly sliced

1 yellow bell pepper, seeded
  and cut into chunks

1 red bell pepper, seeded and
  cut into chunks

1 orange bell pepper, seeded
  and cut into chunks

2 tbsp olive oil

4 garlic cloves

4 fresh rosemary sprigs

pepper

crusty bread, to serve
  (optional)

method

1 Preheat the oven to 400°F/200°C. Prepare the vegetables.

2 Brush an ovenproof dish with a little oil. Arrange the fennel, onions, tomatoes, eggplant, zucchini, and bell peppers in the dish and tuck the garlic cloves and rosemary sprigs among them. Drizzle with the remaining oil and season to taste with pepper.

3 Roast the vegetables in the preheated oven for 10 minutes.

4 Turn the vegetables over, return the dish to the oven, and roast for an additional 10–15 minutes, or until the vegetables are tender and beginning to turn golden brown.

5 Serve the vegetables straight from the dish or transfer to a warm serving platter. Serve immediately with crusty bread, if you like, to soak up the juices.

ratatouille

ingredients

SERVES 4

2 eggplants

4 zucchini

2 yellow bell peppers

2 red bell peppers

2 onions

2 garlic cloves

$2/3$ cup olive oil

1 bouquet garni

3 large tomatoes, peeled,
    seeded, and coarsely
    chopped

salt and pepper

method

1 Coarsely chop the eggplants and zucchini and seed and chop the bell peppers. Slice the onions and finely chop the garlic.

2 Heat the oil in a large pan. Add the onions and cook over low heat, stirring occasionally, for 5 minutes, or until softened. Add the garlic and cook, stirring frequently for an additional 2 minutes.

3 Add the eggplants, zucchini, and bell peppers. Increase the heat to medium and cook, stirring occasionally, until the bell peppers begin to color. Add the bouquet garni, reduce the heat, cover, and simmer gently for 40 minutes.

4 Stir in the chopped tomatoes and season to taste with salt and pepper. Re-cover the pan and simmer gently for an additional 10 minutes. Remove and discard the bouquet garni. Serve warm or cold.

butternut squash stir-fry

ingredients

SERVES 4

2 lb/900 g butternut squash, peeled

3 tbsp peanut oil

1 onion, sliced

2 garlic cloves, crushed

1 tsp coriander seeds

1 tsp cumin seeds

2 tbsp chopped fresh cilantro, plus extra to garnish

generous $1/3$ cup coconut milk

$1/2$ cup water

$2/3$ cup salted cashews

lime wedges, to serve

method

1 Using a sharp knife, slice the butternut squash into bite-size cubes.

2 Heat the oil in a large preheated wok. Add the squash, onion, and garlic and cook for 5 minutes.

3 Stir in the coriander seeds, cumin seeds, and fresh cilantro and cook for 1 minute.

4 Add the coconut milk and water to the wok and bring to a boil. Cover the wok and simmer for 10–15 minutes, or until the squash is tender.

5 Add the cashews and stir to combine. Transfer the stir-fry to warmed serving dishes and garnish with cilantro. Serve with lime wedges for squeezing over.

eggplant gratin

ingredients

SERVES 2

2 onions, finely chopped

2 garlic cloves, very finely
  chopped

2 eggplants, thickly sliced

3 tbsp fresh flat-leaf parsley,
  chopped

$^1/_2$ tsp dried thyme

14 oz/400 g canned chopped
  tomatoes

$1^1/_2$ cups coarsely grated
  mozzarella

6 tbsp freshly grated
  Parmesan

salt and pepper

method

1 Preheat the oven to 400°F/200°C. Heat the oil in a flameproof casserole over medium heat. Add the onions and cook for 5 minutes, or until softened. Add the garlic and cook for a few seconds, or until just beginning to color. Using a slotted spoon, transfer the onion mixture to a plate.

2 Cook the eggplant slices in batches in the same flameproof casserole until they are just lightly browned. Transfer to another plate.

3 Arrange a layer of eggplant slices in the bottom of the casserole dish or a shallow ovenproof dish. Sprinkle with the parsley and thyme, then season to taste with salt and pepper. Add a layer of the onion mixture, tomatoes, and mozzarella, sprinkling parsley, thyme, salt, and pepper over each layer.

4 Continue layering, finishing with a layer of eggplant slices. Sprinkle with the Parmesan. Bake in the preheated oven for 20–30 minutes, or until the top is golden and the eggplants are tender. Serve hot.

cauliflower, eggplant & green bean korma

ingredients

SERVES 4–6

scant ²/₃ cup cashews

1¹/₂ tbsp garlic and ginger
paste

generous ³/₄ cup water

4 tbsp ghee, vegetable oil,
or peanut oil

1 large onion, chopped

5 green cardamom pods,
lightly crushed

1 cinnamon stick, broken
in half

¹/₄ tsp ground turmeric

generous 1 cup heavy cream

6 small new potatoes,
scrubbed and cut into
¹/₂-inch/1-cm pieces

1¹/₂ cups cauliflower florets

¹/₂ tsp garam masala

¹/₂–²/₃ small eggplant, cut into
chunks

5 oz/140 g green beans,
cut into ¹/₂-inch/1-cm
pieces

salt and pepper

chopped fresh mint,
to garnish

method

1 Heat a large flameproof casserole or skillet with a tight-fitting lid over high heat. Add the cashews and stir until they start to brown, then turn them out of the casserole into a spice grinder. Add the garlic and ginger paste and 1 tablespoon of the water and process until a coarse paste forms.

2 Melt the ghee in the casserole over medium–high heat. Add the onion and cook for 5–8 minutes, or until golden brown. Add the nut paste and stir for 5 minutes.

3 Stir in the cardamom pods, cinnamon stick, and turmeric. Add the cream and the remaining water and bring to a boil, stirring. Reduce the heat to the lowest level, cover the casserole, and simmer for 5 minutes.

4 Add the potatoes, cauliflower, and garam masala and simmer, covered, for 5 minutes. Stir in the eggplant and green beans and continue simmering for an additional 5 minutes, or until all the vegetables are tender. Check occasionally to make sure the sauce isn't sticking on the bottom of the pan, and stir in extra water if needed.

5 Taste and adjust the seasoning, adding salt and pepper if necessary. Sprinkle with the mint to serve.

vegetable curry

ingredients

SERVES 4

1 eggplant

1/2 large turnip

12 oz/350 g new potatoes

1/2 small head of cauliflower

8 oz/225 g button
    mushrooms

1 large onion

3 carrots

6 tbsp ghee

2 garlic cloves, crushed

4 tsp finely chopped fresh
    ginger

1–2 fresh green chiles,
    seeded and chopped

1 tbsp paprika

2 tsp ground coriander

1 tbsp mild or medium curry
    powder

scant 2 cups vegetable stock

14 oz/400 g canned chopped
    tomatoes

1 green bell pepper, seeded
    and sliced

1 tbsp cornstarch

2/3 cup coconut milk

2–3 tbsp ground almonds

salt

fresh cilantro sprigs,
    to garnish

freshly cooked rice, to serve

method

1 Cut the eggplant, turnip, and potatoes into 1/2-inch/1-cm cubes. Divide the cauliflower into small florets. The button mushrooms can be used whole or sliced thickly, if preferred. Slice the onion and carrots.

2 Heat the ghee in a large pan. Add the onion, turnip, potatoes, and cauliflower and cook over low heat, stirring frequently, for 3 minutes. Add the garlic, ginger, chiles, paprika, ground coriander, and curry powder and cook, stirring, for 1 minute.

3 Add the stock, tomatoes, eggplant, and mushrooms and season to taste with salt. Cover and simmer, stirring occasionally, for 30 minutes, or until tender. Add the bell pepper and carrots, cover, and cook for an additional 5 minutes.

4 Place the cornstarch and coconut milk in a bowl, mix into a smooth paste, and stir into the vegetable mixture. Add the ground almonds and simmer, stirring constantly, for 2 minutes. Taste and adjust the seasoning, adding salt if necessary. Transfer to serving plates, garnish with cilantro sprigs, and serve immediately with freshly cooked rice.

cauliflower & sweet potato curry

ingredients

SERVES 4

4 tbsp ghee or vegetable oil

2 onions, finely chopped

1 tsp Bengali five-spice mix

1 head of cauliflower, broken
    into florets

1½ large sweet potatoes,
    diced

2 fresh green chiles, seeded
    and finely chopped

1 tsp ginger paste

2 tsp paprika

1½ tsp ground cumin

1 tsp ground turmeric

½ tsp chili powder

3 tomatoes, quartered

2 cups fresh or frozen peas

3 tbsp plain yogurt

1 cup vegetable stock
    or water

1 tsp garam masala

salt

fresh cilantro sprigs,
    to garnish

method

1 Heat the ghee in a large heavy-bottom skillet. Add the onions and Bengali five-spice mix and cook over low heat, stirring frequently, for 10 minutes, or until the onions are golden. Add the cauliflower, sweet potatoes, and chiles and cook, stirring frequently, for 3 minutes.

2 Stir in the ginger paste, paprika, cumin, turmeric, and chili powder and cook, stirring constantly, for 3 minutes. Add the tomatoes and peas and stir in the yogurt and stock. Season to taste with salt, cover, and let simmer for 20 minutes, or until the vegetables are tender.

3 Sprinkle the garam masala over the curry, transfer to a warmed serving dish, and serve immediately, garnished with cilantro sprigs.

parmesan cheese risotto with mushrooms

ingredients

SERVES 6

2 tbsp olive oil or vegetable oil

generous 1 cup risotto rice

2 garlic cloves, crushed

1 onion, chopped

2 celery stalks, chopped

1 red or green bell pepper,
    seeded and chopped

8 oz/225 g button
    mushrooms, thinly sliced

1 tbsp chopped fresh oregano
    or 1 tsp dried oregano

4 cups boiling vegetable stock

$1/4$ cup sun-dried tomatoes in
    olive oil, drained and
    chopped (optional)

$1/2$ cup finely grated
    Parmesan cheese

salt and pepper

fresh flat-leaf parsley sprigs,
    to garnish

method

1 Heat the oil in a deep pan. Add the rice and cook over low heat, stirring constantly, for 2–3 minutes, until the grains are thoroughly coated in oil and translucent.

2 Add the garlic, onion, celery, and bell pepper and cook, stirring frequently, for 5 minutes. Add the mushrooms and cook for 3–4 minutes. Stir in the oregano.

3 Gradually add the hot stock, a ladleful at a time. Stir constantly and add more liquid as the rice absorbs each addition. Increase the heat to medium so that the liquid bubbles. Cook for 15 minutes, then add the sun-dried tomatoes, if using. Cook for an additional 5 minutes, or until all the liquid is absorbed and the rice is creamy. Season to taste with salt and pepper.

4 Remove the risotto from the heat and stir in half the Parmesan until it melts. Transfer the risotto to warmed bowls. Top with the remaining Parmesan, garnish with parsley sprigs, and serve immediately.

risotto with artichoke hearts

ingredients

SERVES 4

8 oz/225 g canned artichoke
    hearts
1 tbsp olive oil
3 tbsp butter
1 small onion, finely chopped
scant 1^1/$_2$ cups risotto rice
5 cups boiling vegetable stock
^{3}/$_4$ cup freshly grated
    Parmesan cheese
salt and pepper
fresh flat-leaf parsley sprigs,
    to garnish

method

1 Drain the artichoke hearts, reserving the liquid, and cut them into quarters.

2 Heat the oil with 2 tablespoons of the butter in a deep pan over medium heat until the butter has melted. Stir in the onion and cook gently, stirring occasionally, for 5 minutes, or until softened and starting to turn golden. Do not brown.

3 Add the rice and mix to coat in oil and butter. Cook, stirring constantly, for 2–3 minutes, or until the grains are translucent.

4 Gradually add the artichoke liquid and the hot stock, a ladle at a time. Stir constantly and add more liquid as the rice absorbs each addition. Increase the heat to medium so that the liquid bubbles. Cook for 15 minutes, then add the artichoke hearts. Cook for an additional 5 minutes, or until all the liquid is absorbed and the rice is creamy.

5 Remove the risotto from the heat and add the remaining butter. Mix well, then stir in the Parmesan until it melts. Adjust the seasoning, adding salt and pepper if necessary. Spoon the risotto into warmed bowls, garnish with parsley sprigs, and serve immediately.

vegetarian paella

ingredients

SERVES 4–6

$^1/_2$ tsp saffron threads

2 tbsp hot water

6 tbsp olive oil

1 Bermuda onion, sliced

3 garlic cloves, minced

1 red bell pepper, seeded
  and sliced

1 orange bell pepper, seeded
  and sliced

1 large eggplant, cubed

1 cup medium-grain paella
  rice

$2^1/_2$ cups vegetable stock

1 lb/450 g tomatoes, peeled
  and chopped

4 oz/115 g button
  mushrooms, sliced

4 oz/115 g green beans,
  halved

14 oz/400 g canned pinto
  beans

salt and pepper

method

1 Put the saffron threads and water in a small bowl or cup and let steep for a few minutes.

2 Meanwhile, heat the oil in a paella pan or wide shallow skillet and cook the onion over medium heat, stirring, for 2–3 minutes, or until softened. Add the garlic, bell peppers, and eggplant and cook, stirring frequently, for 5 minutes.

3 Add the rice and cook, stirring constantly, for 1 minute, or until glossy and coated. Pour in the stock and add the tomatoes, saffron and its soaking water, and salt and pepper to taste. Bring to a boil, then reduce the heat and let simmer, shaking the skillet frequently and stirring occasionally, for 15 minutes.

4 Stir in the mushrooms, green beans, and the pinto beans with their can juices. Cook for an additional 10 minutes, then serve immediately.

egg-fried rice with vegetables

ingredients

SERVES 4

2 tbsp vegetable oil or
   peanut oil

2 garlic cloves, finely chopped

2 fresh red chiles, seeded
   and chopped

4 oz/115 g button mushrooms,
   sliced

2 oz/55 g snow peas, halved

2 oz/55 g baby corn, halved

3 tbsp Thai soy sauce

1 tbsp light brown sugar

a few fresh Thai basil leaves

3 cups rice, cooked and
   cooled

2 eggs, beaten

crispy onion topping
(optional)

2 tbsp vegetable oil or
   peanut oil

2 onions, sliced

method

1 Heat the oil in a wok or large skillet and sauté the garlic and chiles for 2–3 minutes.

2 Add the mushrooms, snow peas, and corn, and stir-fry for 2–3 minutes before adding the soy sauce, sugar, and basil. Stir in the rice.

3 Push the mixture to one side of the wok and add the eggs to the bottom. Stir until lightly set before combining into the rice mixture.

4 If you want to make the crispy onion topping, heat the oil in a separate skillet and sauté the onions until crispy and brown. Serve the rice topped with the onions.